Date Due

NOV 9 1999		
NOV 2 3 1999		
APR 1 9 2003 MAY 0 7 2003		
NOV 2 0 2003		
FEB 1 9 2004		
MAY 1 0 2005		

819.8

Black, A.
Black tie and tales.

2001

PRICE: $26.95 (3559/he)

BLACK TIE AND TALES

ALSO BY ARTHUR BLACK

Black in the Saddle Again

Black by Popular Demand

That Old Black Magic

Arthur! Arthur!

Back to Black

Basic Black

Old Fort William: A History

BLACK TIE AND TALES
ARTHUR BLACK

Published in 1999 by Stoddart Publishing Co. Limited
34 Lesmill Road, Toronto, Canada M3B 2T6
180 Varick Street, 9th Floor, New York, New York 10014

Distributed in Canada by:
General Distribution Services Ltd.
325 Humber College Blvd., Toronto, Ontario M9W 7C3
Tel. (416) 213-1919   Fax (416) 213-1917
Email customer.service@ccmailgw.genpub.com

Distributed in the United States by:
General Distribution Services Inc.
85 River Rock Drive, Suite 202, Buffalo, New York 14207
Toll-free Tel. 1-800-805-1083   Toll-free Fax 1-800-481-6207
Email gdsinc@genpub.com

03   02   01   00   99   1   2   3   4   5

Canadian Cataloguing in Publication Data

Black, Arthur
Black tie and tales

ISBN 0-7737-3193-8

Canadian wit and humor (English).* I. Title.

PS8553.L318B525 1999   C818'.5402   C99-931455-6
PR9199.3.B463B525 1999

Jacket design: Angel Guerra
Text design: Tannice Goddard
Layout: Mary Bowness

We acknowledge for their financial support of our publishing program the Canada Council, the Ontario Arts Council, and the Government of Canada through the Book Publishing Industry Development Program (BPIDP).

Printed and bound in Canada

Contents

Introduction

Another damned thick, square book!
Always scribble, scribble, scribble! Eh! Mister Gibbon?

So spake the duke of Gloucester to the industrious Edward Gibbon upon spying him at work on *The Decline and Fall of the Roman Empire.*

The duke was obviously no book lover, but he raises a good point: who needs another damned thick, square book? Forests are being razed and readers are suffocating under the gross tonnage of volumes, tomes, best-sellers, novels, anthologies, texts, directories, compilations, collections, and catalogues — not to mention the travel books, cookbooks, chapbooks, songbooks, guidebooks, joke books, and how-to manuals being churned out annually in our frenzied Feast of Babble-on. Who needs one more damned thick, square book? More to the point, why should you shell out your hard-earned shekels for *Black Tie and Tales?*

I'd like to advance a number of reasons, the first being that it's not that damned thick and it's definitely not square. More oblongish.

It's also fun. Custom-crafted to take your mind off Quebec separation, gaps in the ozone layer, and the woeful performance of the Toronto Maple Leafs.

In these pages, you'll find discursive essays on themes as various as the dumbing-down of beer, the stinkiest fruit on the planet, the superiority of chopsticks, why you should never give cowboy boots to Indira Gandhi (ask a Hindu), and the exceedingly delicate etymology of prairie oysters (ask a cowboy).

Not to brag, but this is my eighth collection of humorous essays. The first couple of tomes were kind of callow, to tell you the truth.

But I got better with each book. My last one, *Black in the Saddle Again,* won the Leacock Medal for Humour.

And I believe *Black Tie and Tales* is better.

So is this it? Is this as good as it gets?

Probably not. But it's as good as I get — so far.

Next fall, if God is willing and the forests hold, watch for another damned thick, square — but funny — book.

In the meantime, enjoy *Black Tie and Tales* with this personal pledge. If this book fails to make you chortle, chuckle, guffaw, or horselaugh at least a dozen times, simply send me a cheque or money order for the total purchase price (including GST). I promise you'll get a full receipt by return mail.

PART 1

The Little Things in Life

Caution:
Artist/Barber at Work

*The artist brings something into the world that didn't exist
before, and he does it without destroying something else.
A kind of refutation of the conversation of matter.*

JOHN UPDIKE

You know what's particularly wonderful about this country of ours?
Treasures, treasures everywhere. No matter how humble or unlikely
the surroundings.

Take Beardmore, Ontario. Towns don't come much more humble
than Beardmore, with its population of a few hundred souls nestled in
the bosom of northwestern Ontario wilderness about ninety miles due
north of Lake Superior's arched eyebrow.

It's a small town, boasting a couple of gas stations, a general store,
a motel or two — hard to differentiate from any of several thousand
other small Canadian towns. You could drive right down the main
street, past the grocery store and the barber shop, and be back out on
the highway before you knew it. Thousands do, every year.

Ah, but they miss the treasure that way. It's that barber shop on
Main Street. That's where Ewald Rentz lives.

Who's Ewald Rentz? Well, first off, it's Ed to his friends. He was
born in North Dakota, drifted around a bit through Manitoba, but
made his way eventually to Beardmore, where he fell in love with the
land and stayed.

And since all that happened back in 1939, folks take it for granted
that Ed's there for keeps.

In his eighty-odd years Ed has done most of the things a northerner
does. He's been a miner, lumberjack, prospector, cook, and as the
candy-striped pole outside his place attests, a barber.

Oh, yes, and one other thing. Artist. Ed's an artist. World-renowned, as a matter of fact.

There are collectors in England who salivate for his work. Curators from the U.S., Montreal, Toronto, and Vancouver make periodic pilgrimages to the barber shop in Beardmore to see if he's got anything new they can buy. His work is on display in museums across the country, including the National Museum of Man in Ottawa.

Ed Rentz is a national treasure. And the barber in Beardmore.

Ed's what you call a folk artist. He doesn't do abstract impressionist canvasses or mobiles à la Henry Moore. Balsam, birch, and poplar are his media. His inspiration comes from the bush he's wandered through for most of his life.

Ed can pick up a chunk of knotted forest debris that you and I would reject as firewood, turn it over in his own gnarled hands, take it back to his workshop, and with the help of a knife and chisels and judiciously applied dollops of housepaint, transform it into the most exquisite and unexpected bit of art — a ballerina, perhaps. Or a bear cub. Or a Mountie. Or a great spotted fantasy pterodactyl in full flight, with a man on its back, hanging on for dear life.

Ed's tiny barber shop on the main street of Beardmore is crammed full of his works of wonder. Elves, moose, mermaids, wolves, prime ministers . . .

If you're good and he's not too busy, Ed might fetch his step-dance dolls — all meticulously hand-carved — out of their special cloth bags, set them on the floor, haul out his mandolin, and make them dance for you.

But have a care. Just because he's a world-renowned artist and an unusually fine chap of eighty-some winters doesn't mean that Ed's not a working man, too. My, no. If it's a Saturday, you may have to talk to him between haircuts. Ed still knows how to give a haircut.

He still knows how to handle knotty customers too — be they balsam or bushworker.

"One time," says Ed, looking at your correspondent thoughtfully, "a bald guy comes in here. I cut his hair. He gets out of the chair and says, 'Wait a minute. You charged me a buck, the same as these other guys. How come you charge me a buck when I got only a little bit of hair?'

"I told that guy," continues Ed, "'I didn't charge you a buck, I charged you twenty cents to cut your hair.

"'And eighty cents to look for them.'"

4

Benchmark Stenches

Right now, even as you're reading this, David Oren is most likely creeping like a bandit through the Brazilian rain forest. He is stalking an extremely elusive mammal called the mapinguari. A mapinguari is not something you'd like to have in your living room when the vicar comes calling. A mapinguari is a very large, rather nasty, furry ground sloth that has never actually been officially recorded as "present" in modern times. Indeed, most scientists believe the mapinguari became extinct about 9,000 years ago. But Mr. Oren, a U.S. biologist who's been living in and studying the Amazon basin for the past eighteen years, is convinced it's out there, somewhere, munching on the Brazilian underbrush.

He's had dozens of eyewitness reports from natives over the past few years. He's seen with his own eyes large footprints that, he believes, could belong to no other animal. That's why he's out there, padding through the Mato Grosso of the South American outback.

Wearing a gas mask.

Yes, a gas mask. That's the other thing that every eyewitness who's spotted a mapinguari never fails to mention — the stench. "People universally report that this animal really stinks," says Oren. "People become intoxicated and spend a day or two lost in the forest after they come in contact with it."

Interesting to speculate about how bad the mapinguari must smell. Worse than a skunk? As bad as week-old roadkill? More overpowering than Uncle Leroy's outhouse or the breath of your Grade 10 geometry teacher?

How about: worse than the smell of a durian?

The durian is a round green fruit about the size of a watermelon.

The fruit is studded with sharp green spikes and can weigh up to thirty pounds. When you break it open, it reveals white pod-like sections that have the texture of a very ripe Camembert cheese.

But when you break it open, you probably won't notice a thing about the texture. You'll be too busy throwing up. Because the ripe durian smells very much like rotten fish.

That's the bad news about durians. The good news is: you'll probably never smell one. They grow only in Malaysia.

Smells are funny things. My father sold sheep and calves at the Ontario Public Stockyards. It was a job with odiferous overtones. He died thirty-five years ago, but if I close my eyes I can summon up, just as if he were sitting next to me, the aroma of sweat and hay and cowhide and sheepdung that clung to his workclothes.

That's why I smile whenever my city friends recoil in mock horror at the smell of cattle manure. It's perfume to me.

I wish I could say the same about pig manure, but I can't. Pigs don't smell the way other farm animals smell. Cattle are . . . aromatic, horses smell good, sheep smell okay, but pigs stink. Pigs stink in a way that only another pig could forgive. Pigs stink so much that they rated a special seminar at an international agricultural conference held in Ames, Iowa, recently — a two-day seminar devoted to hog odour.

It was enough to take your breath away.

One researcher said she had evidence that the smell from hog lots altered the mood of downwind residents. Another scientist suggested that swine odour could be the cause of disorienting blackout spells. Everyone agreed that the smell of swine was one of the largest remaining hurdles between urban and rural folk.

I pass a couple of hog farms every day on my way to work. Mostly I don't notice the smell, but on the occasions when the wind is just wrong and the car window is open, I am reminded once again of what one microbiologist described as "that indefatigable engine of pollution — the pig."

When that happens, I try to be philosophical about it.

I remind myself that, after all, it could be worse. I could be passing a durian plantation.

I Wouldn't Take
It as a Gift

It was with mixed emotions that I received the news that Aunt Myrtle had passed away. Mixed, because Aunt Myrtle was a sweet, harmless old crone who had never, in eighty-three years, done an intentional nasty to another earthling.

On the other hand, she was responsible for the ugliest present I ever saw.

It was truly hideous: a moose clumsily handcrafted from Lucite, standing on a chunk of paving stone intended to represent a rocky summit somewhere on the Precambrian shield.

And Aunt Myrtle gave it to me as a wedding present.

Which of course meant that I couldn't have the horror melted down into a bowling ball, or leave it out by the curb to await adoption by some passer-by with even lousier taste than Aunt Myrtle.

No, I had to keep the damned thing on the off chance that Aunt Myrtle might drop in and wonder why it wasn't standing over the fireplace.

No more, hurrah. Aunt Myrtle has gone to her reward, and the mutant moose is about to as well, just as soon as I can score a cardboard box big enough to hold it.

Unwanted gifts. Did you ever wonder how much loot we waste on gifts we give to people who hate them? Those fluorescent neckties all dads get at Christmas and on Father's Day? The bottles of perfume you wouldn't use on a skunk-sprayed dog? The plaid socks? The hardcover books even the author's mother wouldn't read? The fondue sets?

The Lucite mooses?

Well, wonder no more. I don't know how much we Canucks throw away on such stuff, but an economics professor at Yale University has calculated that of the $40 billion Yanks spend each year swapping presents back and forth, somewhere between $4 billion and $10 billion is thrown away on stuff the recipient hates on sight — a "deadweight loss" is how Professor Waldfogel describes it.

And it's not just useless gifts. When it comes to ethnic protocol, some gifts are downright offensive.

It is a profoundly bad idea to gift wrap a Black Forest ham for an Israeli, or to give a miniskirt to an orthodox Muslim.

Don't ever give cowboy boots to a Hindu — not if they're made out of cowhide. Cows are sacred beasts in India.

Some gift gaffes are less obvious. You can insult a Japanese businessman by offering him a souvenir letter opener. Symbolically, you're advising him to commit hara-kiri.

And don't show up on a Guatemalan doorstep with a fistful of white flowers. In Guatemala, white flowers are for funerals.

It's an altogether tricky business, giving gifts. It reminds me of the story of Phil Silvers, the American comedian who gained TV immortality as Sergeant Bilko.

Silvers was a very wealthy man, and was reputed to be "the man who has everything." But he had a wealthier friend who was determined to buy Silvers a present that would wow him.

The friend invited Silvers to spend a weekend at his mansion in Beverly Hills. Silvers showed up Friday night at the wheel of a magnificent burgundy Rolls-Royce Silver Cloud.

"My mechanic's not busy this weekend," said the host. "Why don't you let him give your car a little tune-up?" Silvers shrugged assent. Without the comedian's knowledge, his car was whisked away to a garage where a team of experts worked around the clock to install a built-in mahogany bar, a hi-fi system, a colour television, and a VCR.

On Sunday evening, as Silvers was preparing to depart, his host had his renovated car brought around to the front.

"You might want to check out your jalopy," murmured the host, "just to see if it runs any better."

"Ah, who cares?" replied Silvers. "It's only a rental."

Let Us Now Praise (In)Famous Men

If I was to say to you, "Let us now praise famous men," you wouldn't have much trouble coming up with a half-dozen or so names, right?

We've got an impressive list to choose from — Einstein, Edison, Nureyev, Picasso, Bertrand Russell, and Churchill come immediately to mind — and that's without even venturing out of this century.

The same applies to famous women: Marie Curie, Eleanor Roosevelt, Georgia O'Keeffe, Indira Ghandi, Virginia Woolf, and our own Roberta Bondar, to name but six sterling females off the top of my head.

But what if I were to tell you that there is one man who has probably had more of a direct impact on your life than all of the above put together — and what if I were to tell you that you've almost certainly never even heard of him?

Ladies and gentlemen, allow me to introduce Mr. Philo T. Farnsworth.

I know . . . it sounds like the kind of name you'd hear in a comedy sketch on "Hee Haw," but Philo T. Farnsworth was a living, breathing human. A farm boy from Idaho, as a matter of fact. You probably never heard of Farnsworth, but you certainly do know his work.

Farnsworth is the man who gave us television.

Photographing images and transmitting them by airwaves wasn't an idea that originated with Farnsworth. Inventors in France and Britain and the U.S. had been toying with the theory of television for a good half-century before anyone actually sat down and tried to make a working TV set. A German inventor came up with an "imaging machine" away back in 1884. In 1927, a British tinkerer managed to transmit a wavery, almost unrecognizable image from Glasgow all the way to London.

But television as we know it wasn't possible until a twenty-one-year-old Idaho Mormon constructed, tested, and finally patented a "scanning cathode ray tube." Philo T. Farnsworth did just that in 1930. That same year, an engineer working for RCA, the Radio Corporation of America, managed to put together a vastly superior automatic camera. Just a few months later, W2RBX, the world's first experimental television station, went on the air in New York.

If you'd been one of the very few lucky souls with a functioning television transmitter back then, you would have heard — and seen — Kate Smith warbling "When the Moon Comes Over the Mountain."

The era of television was born.

Think for a moment of the TV moguls who owe their careers, not to mention their fortunes, to Philo. Think of the hundreds of millions of dollars that are generated by, and for, NBC, CBS, ABC, CNN, CBC, CTV, to name just a few of the communications giants on this continent.

Would you care to guess what was the very first image that Philo chose to transmit as a test pattern back on that fateful day in 1930? Well, he had to pick a symbol he knew would have instant recognition. Philo may have been a hick, but he was nobody's fool. He chose the dollar sign.

Just think of it — if one Idaho ploughboy had stuck with the family farm instead of monkeying around with a lot of wires and tubes, we might never have had "Bonanza." No "Star Trek." No "Ally McBeal."

But for Philo T. Farnsworth, we might never have heard of Milton Berle or Roseanne or Geraldo.

If Philo T. Farnsworth had been conveniently trampled by a runaway horse in 1926, we wouldn't know the meaning of Andy Rooney, the Home Shopping Channel, Anthony Robbins infomercials, or "Dialing for Dollars."

You owe us big time, Philo.

Murphy's Law

One thing you've got to say for fame: it's certainly democratic. No age restrictions. No race, gender, or political qualifiers. Fame can happen in a heartbeat. It did for Edward A. Murphy, Jr. One moment, Ed was a run-of-the-mill U.S. air force engineer, plugging away at some obscure rocket-sled experiments.

Next moment, he was a household name.

See — way back in 1949, some technician designed sixteen doohickeys to be used in one of Ed Murphy's experiments. Now, there were two ways these doohickeys could be glued in place: a right way and a wrong way. The technician had methodically installed all sixteen the wrong way.

And that's when Edward A. Murphy, Jr. is thought to have shaken his head and said, "You know, if anything can go wrong, it will."

And Edward A. Murphy, Jr. might just as well have hung up his lab smock right there, because with those words he ascended to the pantheon of immortality.

He had unknowingly promulgated Murphy's Law. And what a cottage industry that spawned. Now we have not only Murphy's Law, but also Murphy's Corollarys, Murphy's Faux Pas, and a whole mongrel mix of Murphy maxims for virtually every human misadventure.

Murphy's Corollary Number One states that Murphy's Law may be delayed or suspended for an indefinite period of time, provided that such delay or suspension will result in a greater catastrophe at a later date.

Murphy's Computer Law: No matter how good a deal you get on computer components, the price will always drop immediately after your purchase.

Murphy's Law of Social Behaviour: Light-coloured clothing attracts dark-coloured food spills; dark-coloured clothing attracts light-coloured food spills.

Murphy's Law of Food Preparation: Ovens either overcook or undercook — with the exception of microwave ovens, which always overcook *and* undercook at the same time.

Murphy's Law of Vending Machines: There are only two times when vending machine operators appear: when you kick the machine in disgust, and when you try to wrestle it into giving back your money.

Teachers have their own Murphy's Law. It says that when a teacher is late, the teacher will meet the principal in the hall. If the teacher is late and does not meet the principal, the teacher is late for a faculty meeting.

There are Murphy's laws for musicians, Murphy's laws for dances, Murphy's laws for — there's a Murphy's Law for everything — up to and including love and war.

Murphy's Law of Combat: The only thing more accurate than incoming enemy fire is incoming friendly fire.

And of course the Murphy Combat Law Corollary: Friendly fire . . . isn't.

As for love — well, the original Murphy's Law pretty well covers that, but there are some valuable Murphy addendums. Murphy's Law of Mate Selection: All the good ones are taken. Corollary: If the person isn't taken, there's a good reason.

Murphy's Laws. I don't know whether Edward A. Murphy, Jr. is laughing or crying over his law. You see, Murphy never said Murphy's law. What Murphy said was: "If there are two or more ways to do something, and one of those ways can result in a catastrophe, then someone will do it." Unquote. Which is not quite the same as saying, "Anything that can go wrong, will."

Therein lies the ultimate irony about Edward A. Murphy, Jr. He's world-famous for saying something he never said.

But then, that's just Murphy's Law at work, right?

Oyster Hoisting

Let's hear it for Prairie Oyster — one of the best-kept secrets in Canadian music these days. Prairie Oyster is a Canadian band. They've been around for a couple of decades, making fine music and winning all kinds of awards — Junos and such. But they're not exactly household names, and I'm not sure why that is. I can't figure out why groaners and moaners like Dolly Parton and Billy Ray Cyrus get to cop the C&W glory when there's a group like Prairie Oyster around that can boomachuck them right out of their pointy-toed boots . . . but that's show biz.

Perhaps it's the name. Prairie Oyster. There seems to be some misunderstanding about prairie oysters. Obviously for die-hard fans, some of whom have never seen the prairies — or oysters — Prairie Oyster is the name of one of the best bands in country music.

But to folks of an older generation, a prairie oyster has nothing to do with music. For them a prairie oyster's what you get when you drop a raw egg into a glass of beer or something even stronger. It sounds pretty repulsive, but it's reputed to cure hangovers — at least among those who subscribe to the "hair of the dog" school of imbibing.

However, if you grew up in cattle country — and I'm talking about the cattle country that meanders all the way from the Texas Panhandle north to Alberta's Peace River district — then prairie oysters mean something else again. Among cattlemen, a prairie oyster is . . . well, prairie oysters are . . .

Okay, let me express this as a mathematical equation: one bull, minus two prairie oysters, equals one steer.

Come on, guys, uncross your legs. Prairie oyster production is a necessary part of the cattle business, steer meat being much tastier than bull meat.

The prairie oyster "harvest" happens when most of life's indignities are visited upon ranch cattle — in the fall, at round-up time. That's when calves are herded into holding corrals, roped, branded, vaccinated, dehorned, and . . . relieved of their prairie oysters.

As for *eating* those prairie oysters . . . well, that's not something that was invented by a John Travolta lookalike in leather chaps and a ten-gallon hat. They've been considered culinary treats for centuries. The ancient Romans feasted on prairie oysters, even if they didn't call them that. It's a delicacy — can you think of a more *delicate* delicacy? — that was savoured in the Middle Ages throughout Europe and Asia. And to North American carnivorous connoisseurs, it's a popular dish on this side of the water today.

In the U.S., they call them calf fries, and in season (which is to say, for a week or two right around round-up time) they sell for about six dollars a pound.

Is it gross to eat prairie oysters? Hey, is it gross to eat pig liver? Steak-and-kidney pie? The Chinese serve chicken feet. The Japanese feast on raw octopus. The French salivate for escargot. There isn't much that mankind disdains to put in its mouth. If prairie oysters on a plate are gross, they're in good company.

Besides, it makes sound environmental sense when you think about it. k.d. lang notwithstanding, those calves are going to be separated from their prairie oysters come round-up. What's a cowboy supposed to do with all those savoury little niblets — toss them out for the crows?

No. Not in this age of reuse and recycle. Much better that they end up battered and fried to a crisp.

That way the cowpokes get a tasty, nutritious snack . . . and they aren't left holding the bag.

The Purring of Summer Lawns

I've got a plan for my summer vacation. Two-pronged. For one thing, I'm going to get in shape . . . and at the same time, I'm going to love my neighbours.

It's my front lawn that's going to do it for me. My front lawn grows faster than the national debt and wilder than Don King's hair. It requires regular, systematic, full-frontal assaults. I've been taking care of it the usual way: hauling out the gas mower once a week, yanking the chord, and shredding everybody's eardrums within a quarter-mile, not to mention knocking birds out of the trees with the fumes.

Here's the knock on gas mowers — they're expensive, complicated, noisy, smelly . . . and they pollute like a pulp mill. The California Air Resources Board says running a gas mower for half an hour belches out more emissions than driving a new car 200 miles.

And whoever designed the damned things ought to spend ten years in purgatory strapped to a Toro lawn and garden tractor running at full throttle. Aside from being utterly mufflerless, any lawn cutter who's ever hoisted a ten-gallon can over the thimble-depth gas tank knows what a challenge it is to fill that tank without slopping gas over everything, including yourself. The Environmental Protection Agency reckons that Americans *spill* 17 million gallons of fuel each year just filling small gas-powered engines. Seventeen million gallons! The *Exxon Valdez* spilled only 11 million.

On the plus side, the gas-powered lawn mower is nothing if not democratic. It'll slash through grass, weeds, garden hoses, small mammals . . . even human toes.

Doesn't have to be this way . . . and we don't have to wait for some computer-chipped techno-scientific breakthrough to deliver us.

We already *had* the breakthrough — more than a century and a half ago. That's when a British textile plant foreman, ironically monickered Edwin Budding, unveiled what he called his rotary shearing machine.

We call it the push mower.

The push mower is blindingly simple to operate. You put it on the grass and push on the handles. It cuts the grass. You put it away. No gas, no oil, no carburetor adjustments.

You thought the push mower was extinct? Not quite. Sales fell right off the map back in the 1970s, but they're making a quiet comeback. And in the last ten years, sales of push mowers have tripled.

It's real hard to go deaf with a push mower. Instead of sounding like a Messerschmidt in a power dive, the push mower just . . . purrs. A rhythmic, metallic flutter. Gas-powered mowers remind me of skinheads — angry, aggressive. Push mowers sound like big metal tomcats with a couple of martinis under their belts.

Which brings me to my getting-in-shape plans for the summer. I am not going to buy an $800 NordicTrack or a rowing machine or a Buns of Steel exerciser or a seventy-six-geared mountain bike. I'm heading down to Mouats Hardware this afternoon to pick out a push mower.

Back in 1832, Edwin Budding promoted that first rotary shearing machine thusly: "Country gentlemen will find in using my machine an amusing, useful and healthful exercise."

Well, I'm no country gentleman, and I have my doubts about the "amusing" . . . but I'll go with the rest of Mr. Budding's sales pitch.

Pretty sure my neighbours will too.

Martha, My Close Personal Friend

It came to me the other day as I was hinged over the gaping maw of my car engine with a Gordian knot of battery cables, trying to jump start my car. It came to me that the human brain — this brain, anyway — operates on the same principle as the lint mitt. It picks up fluff, dust, stray hairs like a magnet . . . and lets the big stuff slide right on by. Take battery cables. I can never remember if it's positive to positive or positive to negative.

Take geometry. In high school I studied geometry to death. I knew Propositions 1 through 29 better than I knew my own telephone number. I studied geometry until I had eyes like isosceles triangles and I looked on Pythagoras as a grumpy uncle on my mother's side of my family.

And today? Today I wouldn't know a hypotenuse from a hippopotamus, a congruent triangle from a Concord grape.

Geometrically, my mind is a moonscape. Nothing up there at all.

But I do know that Pearl Jam is a rock group; that O.J. Simpson takes a size-twelve shoe; that twenty-five years ago — not long after I absorbed all that geometry — I came across a sign on an elevator in Barcelona that read in (sort of) English: "The lift is being fixed for the next day. During that time we regret that you will be unbearable."

I know that Russians are the biggest boozers in the world, probably because their domestic vodka is sold with tear-away tinfoil tops. Once you open the bottle, there's no easy way to reseal it. Might as well drink the whole thing.

My point is that all of that knowledge is utterly useless. And I'll have it with me till I die.

But geometry I might conceivably use one day. And I know I'm gonna need to know about the battery cables again come next winter — if not sooner.

And how did I miss Martha Stewart? Am I the only person in the Western world who had no idea who Martha Stewart was?

It was embarrassing. I was at a party, somebody said something about Martha Stewart, everybody else laughed, and I, like a lug, chipped in, "Who's Martha Stewart?"

You'd think I'd said something like, "What's all this about the earth not being flat?" People looked at me with eyes like pie plates, mouths agape. Who's Martha Stewart????? What planet does this guy call home?

I can't help it. Somehow between picking up and filing away all that important data about O.J.'s shoe size, grunge rock groups, Russian bottling technology, and pidgin English notices on Barcelona elevators, I just never got around to hearing about Martha Stewart.

Now I know, of course. I know that she's a TV celebrity, a design-slash-cooking-slash-gardening guru. That she's a regular on "Oprah"; that there's an official Martha Stewart fan club with umpteen thousand signed-up members. I even know that Martha Stewart once climbed Mount Kilimanjaro, and that during the trek she whipped up flambéed bananas and wore La Perla lingerie.

Not as important as knowing about the square on the hypotenuse perhaps, but by cracky I'm ready to put in my two loonies' worth of small talk at the next cocktail party I'm invited to.

Unless, of course, somebody brings up battery cables.

Table Manners

I am not good with chopsticks. I stab and I spear and I skewer and I squeeze and I clamp, but very little food actually makes it from the bowl or platter to my lips. It's an acquired art, eating with chopsticks. And I have yet to acquire it.

But at least I'm not arrogant about it. Not like Giovanni Savasta. Signor Savasta is an international import-export entrepreneur who operates out of the city of Genoa, in Italy. If you plan on visiting Genoa, by the way, you should definitely pack your own dinner cutlery.

See, for the past year, Giovanni Savasta has been assiduously buying up every knife, fork, and spoon he can lay his hands on. He's stockpiling them in a huge warehouse on the outskirts of Genoa while he negotiates with Chinese authorities to have those knives, forks, and spoons shipped to a similar warehouse in Beijing.

Giovanni Savasta figures that Western-style cutlery will be a bigger hit in China than the hula hoop, Cabbage Patch Dolls, and Elvis Presley put together.

As Giovanni less than modestly puts it: "It was so obvious, nobody bothered — nobody but me. I realized that these people ate with chopsticks because they didn't know any better."

All I can say is I hope Giovanni hasn't put a down payment on a villa in Tuscany, because I don't think his brainwave is going to be quite as lucrative as he imagines.

The fact is, we Westerners are pretty much johnny-come-latelies to the knife-and-fork idea ourselves. A couple of hundred years ago, most Westerners — including royalty — were still dipping their grubby paws into common bowls of food and stuffing it into their mouths.

An eighteenth-century English etiquette book sniffs, "When everyone is eating from the same dish you should take care not to put your hand in it before those of higher rank have done so."

Mind you, it was always easy to spot people of noble rank when they gathered around the dinner table. The blue bloods daintily picked out their food using just the thumb and the first two fingers of the right hand. We commoners used both fists.

No one knows how long the Chinese have eaten with chopsticks — their use goes back into the mists of antiquity — but the Chinese don't eat that way because they're too dumb to figure out how to invent cutlery. They do it because they consider our practice of carving food at the table to be primitive and barbaric. The Chinese believe that the mechanics of food preparation should be taken care of in the kitchen, and that meals ought to arrive at the table in portions ready to be eaten.

Besides, there's something naturally elegant about eating with chopsticks. They force the diner to slow down. You can't shovel it in like a furnace stoker the way you can with a fork. You have to take your time and eat modest amounts.

Who knows — you might even indulge in a little conversation.

How civilized.

I remember arguing about chopsticks with a friend who still insists that chopsticks are cruel and unusual punishment for anyone with a healthy appetite. "And those dinky tea cups they give you," he says. "Why the hell can't they put handles on them like normal tea cups?"

Well, I asked a Chinese friend about that, and he smiled and said, "Our cups don't have handles so that we can tell with our hands how hot the tea is. If the tea is too hot for our fingers, we certainly wouldn't want to put it in our mouths."

Er . . . right.

Excuse Me — Has This Water Been Passed?

Call me fixated, but I'm kind of mesmerized by the sixteenth letter of the alphabet.

P, I'm talking about. Urine. Some medical experts recommend drinking urine as a nifty homeopathic manoeuvre. Tantric yogis have been doing it for centuries. Gandhi took regular belts of his own urine and lived to be seventy-nine. Heck, Kevin Costner drank his own pee in the movie *Waterworld*. But then, of course, he was half fish in *Waterworld*. Fish don't have a lot of choice when it comes to urine therapy. They live in the stuff.

Mind you, if Nelson Camus has his way, there might one day be a lot more urine in all of our lives. Mr. Camus unveiled a fairly mind-boggling demonstration at the Invention Convention in Pasadena, California, a few years back. What he had on stage was a hundred-watt floor lamp, a stereo, and a TV, all hooked up to a battery and a clear tank — like a fishtank.

The tank was then filled with a familiar-looking yellow liquid. Camus turned a spigot and the fluid flowed from the tank, through a clear tube, to the battery.

Nothing happened.

For ten seconds. Then suddenly the lamp glowed to life, the stereo started playing Bach, and the TV screen was filled by the face of an announcer reading local news. Sceptics swarmed all over the apparatus looking for a scam, but there was no doubt about it. The appliances were getting their power from the yellow liquid in the tank. And the yellow liquid in the tank was the same yellow liquid we all flush away by the hundreds of millions of tankfuls every day. The answer? The battery. It contained various lithium compounds. Nelson

Camus had discovered that mixing some selected lithium compounds with human urine would create a spunky power source. He says his pee-powered battery, when supplied with five gallons of urine, can produce five kilowatts of power over twenty-four hours. That's enough to provide an average household's energy requirements for four or five days.

Now, please don't write asking for details about Nelson Camus's pee battery. I've told you all I know. I read about it in a Scottish newspaper, the *Glasgow Herald,* about two years ago. Okay, I know one more thing. I know that Camus claims the effluent produced by his battery needs to be filtered only twice to produce clear water.

Well, that's not such a new idea either. Clear water from urine, I mean. You know all the pure, unsullied water in the world? Crystal springs, artesian wells, Lake Louise, the icebergs?

Dinosaur pee.

Not my conclusion. Dr. Milton Grillingham's. The New York scientist says, "Every drop of water we drink has been drunk before and passed as urine." And the overwhelming majority of that water has passed through a dinosaur or two.

Unlikely, you think? Well, don't forget, dinosaurs ruled the earth for about 160 million years. And according to Dr. Grillingham, just one pit stop by just one brontosaurus could last fifty minutes and fill a small in-ground swimming pool.

That's a lot of gallonage.

I don't know how Dr. Grillingham figured that out, and frankly I don't want to know.

I've got enough on my mind with Quebec, my income tax return, and the spectre of Brian Mulroney making speeches in public again. I don't have room for dinosaur kidney function.

Or room for — and you can call me a reactionary — the concept of drinking my urine.

Sorry. Kokanee Lager any time. Dry red wine with a meal. Castor oil if necessary. Even American beer if I have to.

But urine drinking? Sorry. That's an idea I find just a little too tough to swallow.

Please Marry Me (This Is a Recording)

This morning I find myself pondering the predicament (I'm pretty sure it's a predicament) of one Vernon Pierce. Mr. Pierce is a thirty-three-year-old resident of Glendale, Arizona. Pretty good-looking guy — an ex-model, as a matter of fact. Pretty attractive to the ladies too, apparently. At least his wives think so. Yeah, *wives*. Four of them. At once.

That's right. Old sly fox Vernon is currently married to four different women. He also has a few girlfriends, but that's just on the side. How does he do it? Well, his little black book helps. Vernon's book doesn't contain addresses. It contains details of what he's told, and to whom, so he can keep his stories straight. Police also found a small card in his wallet labelled Who to Marry. Clearly, Vernon wasn't finished yet. At least he wasn't until Wife #3 — or possibly #2 — sent the cops to check up on him, and they found themselves knocking on Vernon's door alongside Wife #1. Or maybe it was #4. Vernon's now in the Glendale slammer, doing time for bigamy and fraud. And if he's having conjugal relations, it's probably not with anyone he'd care to make Wife #5.

Still, four wives at once . . . seems a fairly daunting prospect from this vantage point. Not a patch on Tommy Manville, of course. Tommy was the heir to the Johns-Manville fortune, and he spent most of it on wives. He was a serial bridegroom, unlike Vernon. Tommy got married eleven times and divorced ten, each divorce costing him pailfuls of money. Or as Tommy put it, almost poetically, "She cried, and the judge wiped her tears with my chequebook."

And Tommy looks like a wallflower next to the most married man in *The Guinness Book of Records*. That honour goes to Glynn Scotty Wolfe, who got himself hitched to twenty-seven different women.

One after the other. Oh, and that would be *Reverend* Wolfe, by the way. He was a Baptist minister in — oh, well, now it figures — Blythe, *California*.

Ah, but I've been saving the best for last. The most married man — biggest bigamist, if you will — in the monogamous world would have to be Giovanni Vigliotto. Or Nikolai Peruskov. Or perhaps Fred Jepp.

Giovanni, Nikolai, Fred. Those were all names used by one man who got married — are you ready? — 104 times. He tied the knot in twenty-seven different U.S. states and fourteen foreign countries. In 1968 he married four different women on one ocean cruise.

Nobody knows where Giovanni or Nikolai or Fred was born, but the experts agree he died in 1991, serving time, like Vernon — remember Vernon? — for fraud and bigamy.

And here's a still-healthy Vernon Pierce with a measly four wives and a half-dozen or so girlfriends, crying the blues about how hard done by he is. "It wasn't always fun," whines Vernon. "Guys fantasize about something like this, but you don't have your own life."

Oh, yeah, Vernon? Breaking our hearts. Go tell it to Giovanni. Or Nikolai. Or Fred.

There's a Bore Suckered Every Minute

You know what's wrong with *The Guinness Book of Records?* There's no listing for the world's greatest bores. Oh, *Guinness* does the world's greatest river bore (that would be the Hangzhou He River in eastern China, which sports twenty-five-foot waves and a speed of fifteen knots), and *Guinness* does the world's deepest mining bore (that would be the Western Deep Levels Goldmine at Carletonville, South Africa, which goes down 12,391 feet).

But those are not the kind of bores I'm looking for. I'm talking about the human bore. The one who traps you in the elevator or the airport departures lounge. The one who clings like Velcro and weighs like heavy water. The world's biggest human bore. I suspect Dr. Ashley Clarke might well be a contender. He won the Golden Pillow Award back in 1974 as Britain's most boring lecturer. It was his paper "Mechanical Formalism of Emulsion in an Infinite Viscous Medium" that persuaded the judges to give him the — ummm — nod.

Actually, the title alone might have put Dr. Clarke in the winner's circle, but the professor finished his talk with a stunning elocutional triple axel that clinched his victory. "This applies only in an infinite viscous medium," droned the doctor in conclusion. "So in practice it doesn't work at all."

I don't know if Dr. Clarke would be a contender today. I don't even know if he's still a practising bore (although the true professionals don't tend to give it up). But I do know of someone else who is in the running. He is a forty-three-year-old shoe salesman from Omaha, Nebraska — sounds promising already, doesn't he? — by the name of Les Maxton. Les recently submitted his resume to a Most Boring Man Contest run by a magazine. In the resume, Les confesses that he:

- subscribes to eleven industrial and trade journals, including one on fertilizer production and another on eyeglasses;
- collects old tins of floor wax and rubber bands up to, but not longer than, 1.5 inches;
- videotaped every "Lawrence Welk Show" that ever aired on TV, and watches them over and over at least six nights a week;
- likes to polish his black wingtips as he watches the oompahpah man (Les adds that he tries to get in at least seventeen shines a week, in quest of the "ultimate shine").

I'm happy to say that Les Maxton is on his way to world-wide fame and glory. He won that Most Boring Man Contest — and the $5,000 prize that goes with it.

And what does a very boring person do with $5,000 U.S.? Well, he might use it to pick up a few rare early editions of books on screws and nails. Les already has a collection of some 300 such books. Or he might use it to finance a trip he's dreamed of taking since 1987. To . . . Towel City, a textile outlet in North Carolina!

Well, I wish Les Maxton well. I even hope he gets to Towel City. I just hope I don't have to share an airplane seat with him.

If I do, I only hope I can handle it with the aplomb of George Bernard Shaw, who once found himself sitting next to a garrulous young bore at a dinner party. All through the meal, the bore jabbered on relentlessly. Finally Shaw barged in, saying, "You know . . . between the two of us, we know all there is to know."

"Wha— how is that?" asked the bore.

"Well," said Shaw, "you seem to know absolutely everything, except that you're a bore. And I know that."

Where There's Smoke, There's Ire

They try to tell you it can't happen here. Not in Canada. They say that we live in a caring, wealthy society. That we would never abandon our wounded like that. Well, maybe it's true in Kamloops or Kenora or Kapuskasing or Carbonear. Maybe you don't see folks like that on the streets there, but this is the big city, mister, and the big city can grind you up and spit you out like so much budgie gravel. And my eyes tell me different. My eyes tell me that it *does* happen in the big city. I passed them again on my way into work this morning. Pathetic little covens of wasted wretches cowering in doorway after doorway, coughing, rasping, their breath rising in ragged wisps against the chill dawn. . . .

Nah. Little poetic licence there. It's not their breath that's rising. It's cigarette smoke. The refugees I'm talking about are the die-hard smokers — exorcised to the street corners and stairwells outside our schools and offices, factories and assembly plants.

What a change in such a short time! Just a few years ago, the workplace was *bathed* in cigarette smoke. There were ashtrays in every office cubby-hole. Today? Well, I don't know what it's like where you work, but in this building if somebody lit a cigarette I think they'd be treated as if they were having some kind of a hydrophobic fit. Smoking is out. And smokers are on the run.

The war against smoking rages on . . . and not just where you and I work. Recently, tobacco — even chewing tobacco — was outlawed by Major League Baseball officials — a ruling that also applies to every minor-league club in North America.

Not long after, the Canadian navy became the world's first armed service to ban the sale of tobacco to personnel. No smoking aboard

Canadian ships while in port. If a sailor wants a smoke at sea he/she has to go on deck. Typhoon? Too bad.

Could be worse for smokers. They could live in Davis, California. Davis is officially reckoned to be the toughest smoking venue this side of a live ammunition dump. In Davis, you can get arrested for smoking indoors in any public building — and also outdoors within twenty feet of a doorway or a public service area, such as a bus stop or a pay telephone booth.

The Niconarcs of Davis aren't entirely heartless, however. They will let you smoke in a public park. As long as you keep moving — and providing you're not within ten feet of anyone else.

Hey. It could be tougher still. You could be in jail in McPherson County, Kansas. The McPherson lock-up is a — you guessed it — a smoke-free facility. They might hang you at McPherson, but they sure don't want to hear a cigarette cough on your way to the gallows.

Sheriff Larry Powell says it hasn't been a — ahem — walk in the park, enforcing the tobacco ban at McPherson. "Seems like every prisoner we get in here smokes," he says. "Some of them told me they'd think twice about committing a crime in this county for fear of being locked up without their cigarettes."

Desperate cons resort to desperate measures. Sheriff Powell got wind of prisoners hoarding spinach from their meals, drying it out, wrapping it in toilet paper, and lighting these roll-yer-owns by sticking chewing gum foil into electrical sockets.

A jump-started spinach cigarette. I've heard of walking a mile for a Camel, but this is ridiculous.

Larry Powell didn't get to be sheriff of McPherson County by being a patsy. He's ordered that all weeds growing in the exercise area are to be pulled up and confiscated . . . and he's banned spinach from the prison menu.

Seems a little harsh — even for a penal institution. You'd think the jailers and the inmates could reach some reasonably amicable compromise. I bet the boys would be more than happy to eat up all their spinach if the screws would just bend a little . . . let 'em have a tiny cigarette break every now and then.

And hey, if it's second-hand smoke Sheriff Powell's worried about, I'm sure the inmates would be more than happy to step outside to take their break.

Harvesting Moons

Ever been mooned?

I was . . . two days ago. Middle of the afternoon, I'm standing on the north side of Wellington Street in downtown Toronto the Uptight, waiting for a hole in the traffic so I can get to the south side of Wellington Street. A car goes by, station wagon maybe. I don't pay a lot of attention, except that out of the corner of my eye I see this enormous pink head in the rear window as the car passes. I remember thinking, Huh, pink balloon, Easter celebration. And then the penny dropped. Not a pink balloon. I had been mooned.

Odd way to spend your leisure hours when you think about it — mooning people. I mean, because of logistics the mooner doesn't even get to see the facial reaction of the moon-ee. Maybe they've got a follow-up car with a Camcorder out the window. I sure hope so.

Mooning. I wonder how long it's been around as a means of, uh, expression, I guess. I remember it hit the headlines in a big way about ten years ago, when the Queen visited New Zealand. Maori warriors protested her presence by shooting a few moons during the royal walkabout. But I think mooning was around long before that. I seem to remember it, along with streaking, as a college fad way back in the sixties.

Kinda thought it had died out there, but my newspapers tell me differently. They tell me about a Mexican disc jockey by the name of Pedro Rego who indirectly mooned a good part of the country. He told his radio audience that all those who pulled down their bosses' pants and brought them to the station would get a cheque for $5,000 (U.S.). Involuntary mooning, I guess you'd call that. Pedro's station manager called it *dumbissimo* and suspended the deejay without pay pending an investigation. Story doesn't say how many pairs of pantaloons were turned in.

Things went a little tougher for Lorenzo Chavez of Rio Negro, Argentina, late last year. Chavez was in a bank line-up at Argentina's Gran Banco National, a line-up that, like most bank line-ups, was creeping along at the speed of the Wisconsin Glacier. Chavez could see the bank's security camera staring back at him. He was bored. He winked at the camera. He stuck out his tongue at it. He crossed his eyes at it. And then . . . he mooned it.

Argentinian bankers are not known for their sense of humour. Neither are Argentinian judges. Chavez was arrested, charged, tried, found guilty, and sentenced. To five years in jail. For mooning.

Which is stupid. Chavez is appealing, and I suspect he'll get off with a light fine.

All he has to do is find a judge with a Christian sense of charity. Willing to turn the other cheek.

Gum That's Good for You?

"We condemn . . . the rubbery abomination. It will exhaust the salivary glands and cause the intestines to stick together."
ANONYMOUS DOCTOR, 1869

"Hey, Joe . . . you got chewing gum?"
ANONYMOUS KOREAN POW, 1951

Good old gum. Our gift to civilization. And we didn't even invent it.

That honour must go to the natives of Mexico, who for long generations were in the habit of gathering gum from the chicle tree and tucking it in their mouths to keep their throats moist during overland treks.

An American photographer by the name of Thomas Adams discovered the glop during a trip to Mexico in the mid-nineteenth century. He brought a mess of it back to the United States and spent several months trying unsuccessfully to render it into commercial rubber. One day, in a state of frustrated absent-mindedness, he stuck a dab of the goo in his mouth and started chewing it — just as Mexicans had been for several centuries.

Adams discovered that he liked it.

He called up a businessman and tried to interest him in the idea of selling "chewing gum." The businessman looked at Adams as if he was out of his mind.

Undeterred, Thomas Adams started his very own chewing-gum business. Before long, he had a six-storey factory with 250 employees, all dedicated to the manufacture and distribution of chewing gum.

Adams was on his way to becoming a multimillionaire. But he never forgot the origin of his personal Klondike — the humble Mexican chicle tree.

Which is why, nearly a hundred years later, we still buy Adams's Chiclets.

And not just Chiclets — Dentyne, Wrigleys, Big Red, Beechnut, Excel, Trident, Clorets, and Dubble Bubble as well.

Humankind has been chewing gum (and expectorating unsightly blobs of it) all over the world since old Tom Adams first put it on the market back in 1872. Who can estimate the uncountable tons of hardened chaw that have festooned the bottoms of theatre seats, classroom desks, and restaurant tables from Manitouwadge to Mandalay?

It has not been universally loved. A suspiciously puffy cheek would earn you six of the best from my Grade 6 teacher, Mr. Hewitt. In Singapore, you can still go to jail for chewing gum in public.

But the very worst thing I know about chewing gum is that it has . . . become respectable.

A dental scientist by the name of Carl Kleber has developed a gum that contains minute abrasives that grind against the surface of your teeth as you chew.

Just like toothpaste.

Dr. Kleber's gum actually cleans and polishes your teeth as you chew it.

Not surprisingly, Dr. Kleber had no shortage of guinea pigs to test his gum.

"You can get monkeys to chew gum," he says, "but only for a couple of minutes. After that, they just take it out and stick it in their hair."

No such problem with the elementary school pupils who first tried Dr. Kleber's healthy chewing gum. They worked for free.

"What they really enjoyed," says Kleber, "was being able to chew gum in school."

Healthy gum. Chewing allowed right in class.

Mr. Hewitt must be turning over in his grave.

Birds and Bees?
Hold Your Horses!

Geez, how do I get myself into these things? I've agreed to emcee a festival — a Festival of Erotica. Erotic poems read by a dozen or so erotic-poem writers. Erotica. What do I know from erotica?

Lorna Crozier's gonna be there. John Gray's gonna be there. Bill Richardson will be *double entendring* all over the stage, and so will Cathy Ford and Susan Musgrave. Each and every libidinous one of them positively oozing innuendo.

Only one question — what the hell am I doing in the mix?

I'm not some post-modernist libertine who runs around dressed in a toga and a laurel wreath quaffing Kelowna red out of a ram's horn, for crying out loud.

I am a child of the fifties . . . which is to say, repressed, dampened, beaten down. Sexual revolution? What sexual revolution? I grew up in the era of brush cuts, cold showers, and Pat Boone, for mercy's sake. I don't celebrate sexual openness. Are you kidding? I don't even mention it. I may *think* about it seventeen hours a day, but I don't mention it.

Somebody once asked Woody Allen if sex was dirty. He answered, "Only if it's done right." Well, exactly.

And I'm hosting a Festival of Erotic Poetry??????

I am not worthy. I am not worthy.

You want to hear about my sex education? It took place in a gravel pit. My brother-in-law arranged for me — a callow, hormone-besotted twelve-year-old — to witness the mating of a buckskin palomino mare and a stallion.

You will not find any love poems by Richard Lovelace or Sir John Suckling limning the glories of horses mating. It is not what you'd call a display of lyrical gentility. It is more along the lines of the Nazi blitzkrieg of Poland.

Besides, have you ever — you know — seen a stallion when it's . . . hot to trot?

I felt totally inadequate for the next thirty-five years.

It took me a long time to get sex in its proper perspective — which is to say, firmly in the rumpus room of life. Nobody ever said it better than Lord Chesterfield did in a letter to his son: "The pleasure is momentary," huffed the lord, "the position ridiculous, and the expense damnable."

That's why when it comes to sex education, I vote for subterfuge, equivocation, fantasy, and outright lying.

If I'd had a choice, I would have taken hands down the old stork-in-the-chimney, foundling-under-the-cabbage-leaf approach over the thunder and whinnying of equine coitus.

When it comes to introductions to sex, I would have preferred the one that Laurence Olivier's son got at Brighton Beach. The Oliviers, *fils et père*, were strolling along the seashore with Noel Coward when they came upon two dogs doing . . . what dogs have a penchant for doing at the most inopportune times. The young lad inquired as to what was going on. "It's like this, dear boy," explained Coward. "The one in front is blind and the kind one behind is pushing him."

I would even have settled for the elegant mystery of the explanation conferred upon a young French lad, who asked his father, "When you went on your honeymoon with Maman in Italy, where was I, Papa?"

The French father thought for a moment, then leaned back and murmured urbanely, "Why, you went there with me, and came back with your mother."

Sex: Bad for the Eyes

Okay. I had no trouble accepting that cigarettes could kill me dead. And I didn't need to be a Rhodes Scholar to figure out that too much booze would fricassee my kidneys and turn my liver into Silly Putty.

I even grew resigned to the fact that bacon was life-threatening; that simple, wholesome culinary pleasures like eggs, butter, and sirloin steak could transform me into a walking toxic-waste site.

But now, by God, they've gone too far.

They've announced that sex can make me blind.

I'm serious! You can read all about it in the June edition of *Archives of Ophthalmology,* which is published by the American Medical Association.

Researchers studied half a dozen patients — five men and one woman — all of whom, instead of opting for the traditional postcoital cigarette, hollered for an eye chart. They couldn't see, they claimed. Or if they could, they couldn't see much.

The researchers have a name for the disorder — valsava retinopathy. Previously, victims of VR fell afoul of the condition by decidedly less interesting avenues. Doctors traditionally associated valsava retinopathy with severe vomiting, prolonged coughing, or weightlifting.

Now they're saying you can get it through sex.

That's the bad news. The good news is that the blindness or blurred vision is temporary. Of the six patients, four got their vision back in a matter of days with no treatment. The other two needed laser surgery to seal tiny rips in the tissues at the backs of their eyes.

But all of them got their eyesight back and are free to read eye charts — or to have sex — to their hearts' content.

Reminds me of an old joke. You know, the one about the famous, silver-tongued preacher whose sermons were known to enthral the congregation to the point of rapture. One Sunday the preacher was orating away, charming the faithful. A shapely woman in the balcony leaned over, eager to hear his every honeyed word. She leaned over farther and farther . . . until finally she fell right out of the balcony.

But Providence intervened, and as she plunged precipitously towards the ground-level pews, her ankle was caught in a chandelier. And there she dangled, safe from injury but with her undergarments grievously exposed to the view of everyone in the church.

The minister, who was nothing if not quick-witted, immediately thundered: "Whosoever gazes upon yon lamb of the church will immediately be struck blind!"

There ensued a few seconds of agonized silence . . . until a voice from the back of the church rasped: "I believe I'll risk one eye."

Funny? Even the Corpse Was Smiling

Laughter is an orgasm triggered by the intercourse of reason with unreason.

JACK KROLL

Humour can be dissected, as a frog can, but the thing dies in the process and the innards are discouraging to any but the scientific mind.

E.B. WHITE

Ever stop to think how strange a phenomenon is the common, garden-variety laugh?

Call it a chortle, a snicker, a guffaw, a whoop, a chuckle, or a giggle, it sneaks up on you unawares and slam-dunks you without warning. Suddenly, your belly is shaking, the corners of your lips are heading for their respective ears, and you are, whether you want to or not, laughing.

But why? Trying to define exactly what is funny is like trying to braid a rope out of smoke. One man's Wayne is another man's Shuster. Some people think David Letterman is the funniest man on the planet. Others think he's a tiresome, nasty smart-ass.

Some people love the Three Stooges. Others line up for Victor Borge.

And the French?

The French actually believe that *Jerry Lewis* is funny.

More — they think he's a comedic genius. They've honoured him with the Gallic equivalent of a knighthood. The French look at his cross-eyed, knock-kneed, buck-toothed, half-witted screen persona and they fall in *les aisles*.

Go figure.

Canadians? It's hard to say exactly where Canadians fit in the pantheon of humour. We have Stephen Leacock, of course. And there aren't too many writers funnier than W.O. Mitchell or Bill Kinsella when they put their jester caps on. And we export a very high grade of comic artist. Rich Little, John Candy, Dan Ackroyd, Dave Thomas, Martin Short, Jim Carrey — Canucks to a man. But "export" is the operative word. None of those comics got famous in Canada. They had to go south for certification.

Maybe they should have gone to Japan. My spies tell me that a brand-new religion is sweeping the Land of the Rising Sun. It's called Taisokyo. The only commandment in the Gospel according to Taisokyo is that you must laugh. At everything. That includes floods, fires, famine, bankruptcy, disease, and traffic accidents. The two million Japanese who follow Taisokyo can be kicked out of the church for *not* laughing uproariously at death and disaster.

Your typical Taisokyo funeral is not quite what you'd see down at the local cathedral or synagogue, either. Funeral guests come with cream pies to push in the faces of mourning family members. Says one Taisokyo disciple, "If we feel like it, we draw a mustache on the face of the corpse and even set fire to the casket."

I guess you have to be there. . . .

And then there's Britain's entry into the humour sweepstakes.

His name is Magnus. He's a computer created by a team of twenty computer engineers at Imperial College in London.

But Magnus is not your average battery-run agglomeration of wire and plastic and silicon chip. The boffins who created Magnus claim to have built a "neural-computer brain" very close to the one we all carry around on our shoulders.

Magnus thinks, suffers emotions, and even dabbles in free will, say his creators.

Aha, but can Magnus take a joke? More to the point can Magnus *tell* a joke?

Igor Aleksander, the engineer in charge, admits that Magnus is no, well, Charlie Farquharson.

"If you ask Magnus to tell you a joke," he says, "it may say, 'Okay, here is a joke.' Then it will say, 'Now can we get back to business?'"

Yeah, well. The French would probably eat it up.

PART 2

You Speak English?

Can We Talk?

Language is a form of organized stutter.

Marshall McLuhan

McLuhan was right. Every syllable of spoken word we know, from Hamlet's soliloquy on the battlements to Jean Chrétien's sound bites on "Prime Time News" — nothing but organized stutter.

How did that come to be? Nobody knows precisely when Grok the caveman grew tired of waving his hairy arms around and decided to use grunts, growls, and snorts to express himself, but anthropologists know that the human throat was capable of speech anywhere from 20,000 to 35,000 years ago, so it's a safe bet that we nattered at each other for several thousand years before somebody got a bright idea and said, "I say, chaps, how be we call all these noises we're making 'English'?"

And not just English. There are some 9,000 languages and dialects spoken around the world. The most popular is Mandarin Chinese. English is second, then Hindi, Russian, and Spanish.

Ottawa Valley Speak is not in the top one hundred.

Not all languages are spoken, either. The deaf and the mute have sign language. Boy Scouts and aircraft-carrier signalmen use semaphore. Various Indian tribes used to communicate by smoke signal. There is Morse code, Braille, NHL referee hand signals. . . .

And there is the drum.

Most of us in North America don't consider the drum to be a primary source of communication among human beings. For us, the drum is a loud, rather tiresome, quasi-musical instrument employed to drown out other musicians. It owes its current popularity to Mr. Ringo Starr, a large-nosed Liverpudlian who regularly assaulted a drum kit on behalf of the Beatles.

But we in North America don't know diddly-squat about drums.

They do in West Africa. The Akan people, who are found throughout the West African countries, have been using drums to talk with each other for centuries. Very effectively too. A good West African drummer can pound out a message that will carry for nearly forty miles. That message will in turn be picked up by other drummers, in all directions, each of whom will transmit it to his "listening audience."

In hours a message can sweep across thousands of miles without benefit of telephone poles, highways, or communications satellites.

How does a drum message "read"? Not cut and dried like Morse code. More like a soliloquy. West African drumspeak is highly poetic and beautiful. A plane crash translates as "A canoe that flies like a bird has fallen out of the sky." When the much-revered president of the Ivory Coast died a few years back, the tribal drums throbbed out a dirge that translated as "The great elephant has lost its teeth. The leopard has lost its spots. The baobab [tree] has crashed down."

A little more majestic than "Kennedy shot!" wouldn't you say?

Reminds me of my most memorable encounter with a nonspoken language. Actually, it was a second-hand encounter. I heard the story from two wandering Canucks I met on a Spanish freighter waddling along the west coast of Africa. The two Canadians had been living on the island of Gomera, a tiny, volcanic atoll among the Canary Islands. They told a story of climbing one of the many rugged mountains on the island.

What they couldn't understand was how every villager they met seemed to be expecting them. Odd, considering they were climbing a goat path and there were no roads or telephones on their route. When they reached a village on the top of the mountain, they were astounded to find that the townsfolk had killed and cooked a goat in their honour. Yes, the head man told them, they'd been expecting "two foreigners." "Bienvenido."

But how? How could they know?

The two Canucks were masters of suspense. They waited until I paid for a round of drinks in the ship's saloon before they explained.

It was whistling. The people on the island of Gomera speak a language of whistles called *silbo*. The piercing whistles carry so well across valleys (or up mountains) that a "speaker" can be heard up to five miles away.

I wonder what Marshall McLuhan would say about that.

Larking About

The French poet Paul Valéry once said a pretty smart thing on the subject of looking at things. I mean *really* looking at things. "To look," said Valéry, "is to forget the names of the things you are seeing."

I think I know what he means. I used to hike with a biologist pal until I couldn't stand it any more. We'd be walking along and maybe a big red-tailed hawk would swoop across the sky. "Wow, did you see that?" I'd babble.

"*Buteo jamaicensis,*" my biologist would murmur smugly. "Immature male."

He was always like that. He never saw that Lily Tomlin thing that rabbits do with their mouths, or the Picassoesque dance of a monarch butterfly across a meadow, or the saucy "up yours" semaphore of a disappearing white-tailed rump. He saw *Danaus plexippus* and *Odocoileus virginianus*. Which are the correct terms for a monarch and a white-tailed deer — all very true and scientifically accurate, but . . . kind of unfulfilling.

It's perplexing for me, because as a writer, I want to know the names of things.

Which is where one of my favourite books comes in. It's a skinny one, called *An Exaltation of Larks*. The author, James Lipton, has brought together some of the wonderful collective terms the English language has for things like . . . well, like a gaggle of geese, a school of fish, a pride of lions, a flock of sheep.

Lesser-known, almost-forgotten terms too. Like a leap of leopards, a sounder of swine, a rafter of turkeys, and a kindle of kittens.

And some terms so beautiful, so apt, it's hard to imagine how we ever let them slip out of usage. How about a murmuration of starlings?

A bouquet of pheasants? A knot of toads? A hover of trout? A peep of chickens? And perhaps best of all, the title of the book — an exaltation of larks?

James Lipton is still alive, and still collecting collectives. Inventing them too. He's got a new book out, *An Exaltation of Business and Finance*. (I know . . . it doesn't exactly sing, does it?) But I think Lipton wrote *Exhaltation Two* with tongue firmly lodged in buccal cavity. He's having a lot of fun collectivizing the business world of the late twentieth century.

His collective term for a group of accountants? Why, a column, of course. Similarly, he gives us a riddle of economists, a flush of plumbers, a drove of cabbies, a slouch of models, a pound of pianists, and a lot of realtors.

Not to mention a nucleus of physicists, a rash of dermatologists, and — in recognition of all those casting couches in Hollywood — a pinch of producers.

Lipton carries on a game that English speakers have been playing with the language for at least 600 years. It's a game anyone can play with any degree of bite. Lipton also offers an odium of politicians, an unction of undertakers, a glaze of tourists, a grope of groupies, and a shrivel of critics.

Well, no shrivels from this critic. Make it a bushel basket of thank-yous to James Lipton for reminding us what fun our language can be. And always has been.

An Exaltation of Larks. Try it. It's, well, a barrel of laughs.

Joking Newfies

Canada's thirteenth prime minister, John George Diefenbaker, probably had the healthiest attitude towards public-opinion polls. Back in the early 1960s a reporter asked the Chief what he thought of a newspaper poll that showed his popularity was on the wane.

Diefenbaker, eyes blazing, looked down at the reporter and thundered, "Poles? Poles? You know what dogs do to poles!"

And fair comment too. The trouble with polls is that they are mostly wrong, irrelevant — or they tell you things that anyone with the IQ of a cauliflower already knows.

Take this recent *Maclean's* magazine poll. "Newfoundlanders Are Canada's Busiest Lovers," it shrieks.

Yeah . . . so?

Is this supposed to be a surprise? The pollsters thought perhaps that retirees in Victoria or brokers on Bay Street could seriously challenge residents of the Rock when it comes to *amour*?

I thought everybody knew that Newfoundland was the love nest of the Canadian psyche. I mean, look at the place names!

Take a short drive up the east coast of Trinity Bay, and before you can say I'se the Bye you'll find yourself passing through a trio of hamlets called Heart's Delight, Heart's Desire, and Heart's Content.

Toronto has the Frederick G. Gardiner Expressway. Newfoundland has Tickle Cove.

British Columbia has Richmond and Comox and Surrey.

Newfoundland has Bareneed and Ha Ha Bay and Nancy Oh.

And that's without even getting into the lascivious Newfoundland place names — names like Cupids and Spoon Cove. Leading Tickles and Conception Bay. Comfort Cove. Breakheart Point. Happy Valley.

Goose Bay. Not to mention Dildo, Dildo Arm, Dildo Cove, Dildo Islands, Dildo Pond, Dildo Run, and South Dildo.

And, of course, Come by Chance.

Pretty hard to be a puritan when you're living in a suggestible landscape like that.

Some Newfoundlanders claim it's the seafood diet that gives them their sexual stamina. Others say it's the combination of isolation and even tougher than usual economic times that account for the popularity of mankind's oldest indoor sport.

I think it might be something else.

Anyone who's ever visited Newfoundland cannot fail to notice that the residents there still cling to something that the rest of us seem to have misplaced.

I don't know what to call it. It seems to be made up of generous dollops of innocence, genuine friendliness, innate kindness, and an unsinkable urge to enjoy life. Which they do, in spite of a grim climate, an unforgiving ocean, a moribund economy — and the stupid Newfie jokes the (secretly envious) rest of Canada tells about them.

You want a Newfie joke? I'll tell you one. I heard it in a bar on Duckworth Street one night when a raucous table of "Come from Aways" was filling the smoky air with Newfie jokes.

It went on for a while until finally the waiter, a brawny Bayman, came over to the table, put down his tray, and leaned on our table on his two hairy fists.

It looked like trouble. Until he opened his mouth.

"There was a Toronto feller came here to live in Sin Jahn's t'ree years ago," he told us. "After a couple of months he noticed a strange t'ing while he was shavin' one morning. He had this brown ring runnin' right across his forehead. Well, sir, he rushed right down to the emergency ward of the hospital. The doctor examined the ring on his forehead. Didn't say a word. The feller wit' the ring said, 'What is it, Doctor? Is it serious?' The doctor looked at him and said, 'You're from Toronto, are ye?'

'That's right!' said the feller wit' the ring. 'But how could you know that? And what is this brown ring, anyway?'

"'Tis nothing to worry about,' said the doctor. 'You're merely full of shit and down a quart.'"

And then the waiter bought us a round of beer.

Guerrilla Kindness

Today I would like to launch a full-frontal assault on the most insidious phrase in the English language.

The phrase is: "Haveaniceday."

Everybody slings it at you. Postal clerks. Traffic cops. Shoeshine persons. Used-car salesmen. Ice-cream vendors. Bus drivers. Matchbooks. Cocktail napkins.

Haveaniceday.

There was a judge in Cortland, New York, who recently sent a crook to the slammer for seven years with the following summation: "You are hereby remanded to the custody of the sheriff's department for delivery to the custody of state officials. Have a nice day."

Which, for me, is a perfect illustration of why the phrase has got to go.

It doesn't mean anything.

People who tell you to "Haveaniceday" couldn't really care less if you got hit by a Greyhound bus once you were out of their sight. It's a kiss-off phrase. What it really means is "Next!"

Haveaniceday. One of the few soft spots in an otherwise magnificent language. The French say *au revoir*. The Spanish send you on your way with *hasta la vista*. The Germans wish you *auf Wiedersehen*. And the Italians bid you a magnificent tongue-tumbling *arrivederci*.

And what do we say? We say, "Haveaniceday."

Such a wussy, smile-button, Ronald McDonald-style benediction.

Maybe the problem is the very word "nice."

When we swiped the word from the French back in the thirteenth century, "nice" connoted foolishness, senselessness. After a couple of hundred years, "nice" came to mean elegant — in a show-offy kind of way. Later, "nice" could mean lazy, effeminate, tender, or subtle, depending on the linguistic whim of the day.

"Nice" has been around the block a few times, and there are some folks in London, England, who would like to put it into permanent retirement. Ray Chandler and Jo Ellen Grzyb run a course called The Nice Factor. They charge students the equivalent of $300 Canadian to loosen those stiff British upper lips and sharpen their tongues. They teach executives, housewives, lawyers — whoever needs it — not to be so dashed diffident.

In other words, stop being so bloody "nice" all the time.

"The disease of niceness cripples more lives than alcoholism," claims Chandler, and perhaps he's right. His partner, Grzyb, says she's a recovering nice person. "I was so nice I used to apologize to plants and sofas that I bumped into."

Chandler and Grzyb aren't trying to turn out social commandos ready to stomp with jackboots where they used to cringe and cower.

"We are not against being nice itself, but we try to help people who are *always* nice — even to people who do not deserve it — and whose lips always say yes when their minds say no."

Well, I suppose some folks could use such a course. But it's sad that we need a course to teach people how to be less generous.

I much prefer the rumours I hear of an underground movement that's flickering across North America right now. Near as I can tell, this movement was born in the brain of Gavin Whitsett, a professor of communications at the University of Indiana.

Whitsett engages in what he describes as "random acts of senseless kindness." He buries nickels in sandboxes for kids to find. He clips coupons for foodstuffs he doesn't want and leaves them anonymously on the shelves of his local supermarket. He takes his Polaroid camera to the park or the beach and snaps pictures of happy families or couples in love — then gives them the photo.

No charge. No here's-my-business-card. No we-must-do-lunch.

Just . . . guerrilla kindness.

Whitsett defines it as "doing unexpected, kind things for other people, whether you know them or not."

Imagine. Actually being nice instead of chanting, "Haveaniceday."

Can you imagine what a world this would be if we all caught Gavin Whitsett's disease?

Catch you later. I'm off to bury a few nickels.

Dead Heads

So what do you think of that headline? Good? Bad? Ho-hum? Well, don't blame me — I didn't write it.

Headlines are an interesting phenomenon. Imagine you were handed a story of say 750 to 1,000 words by an editor with a cigar butt stuck in his beak, who removed the cigar just long enough to growl, "Here, punk — put a headline on this."

You know that you've got four, five, maybe half a dozen words to sum up the story. What do you write?

If you're like most headline writers, nothing very interesting. *New Republic* magazine recently asked its readers to submit their idea of the most boring headlines they'd seen.

The magazine was inundated.

"New Zealand: Laboratory for Air Transport Development," read one entry.

"Astronaut Gets Dead Newt Out of Tank" was another.

The *Charleston Gazette* submitted "Tourist Bureaus May Consolidate, But Not Right Now."

This was challenged by an offering from an Atlanta paper: "Local Earthquakes Rarely Noticed."

The *New Haven Register* weighed in with "State May Allow Drivers to Put Sticker in Window" — while the *New York Times* alerted its readers that "Professors in 14-Nation Study Say Their Ideas Are Ignored."

Chicago readers of the *Daily Southtown* were no doubt paralyzed to learn that "Case Hinges on Evidence."

Interestingly enough, Canadian entries made up a fair proportion of the submissions. "Many Ignore Canada's Day of Independence," lamented the *Fort Lauderdale Sun-Sentinel,* while the *Seattle Post-Intelligencer* harrumphed, "Canadian Wheat Blamed."

Canada's own *Globe and Mail* — the newspaper that is pleased to pronounce itself Canada's "national" newspaper — hastened to inform the world at large: "Canadians Content, Survey Finds."

I wish the *New Republic* survey had acknowledged other headline categories — cleverest headline, for example. I've always admired the show-business paper *Variety* for the shrewd conciseness of its headlines. Once, when a blizzard paralyzed Buffalo and would-be theatre-goers, *Variety* summed up the situation with "Bliz Boffs Buff Biz."

Another time, when surveys indicated that rural audiences did not flock to movies whose themes were rural or agricultural, *Variety* boiled it down to this headline: "Stix Nix Hix Pix."

Remember when Washington announced it would no longer bail out New York City financially? The *New York Post* summed up the situation pithily with "Feds to New York: Drop Dead."

There are a lot of headline categories *New Republic* could have honoured — how about Most Unintentionally Hilarious Headline? There's a bagful of entries in this department — how about "Father of Nine Fined $100 for Failure to Stop"?

Or this headline in the *New York Herald*: "Dead Policeman on Force 23 Years."

The Baltimore editor that OK'd this headline may never live it down: "Florist Asks Girls To Drop Strapless Gowns."

And how would you like to be an editor on the San Francisco newspaper that ran this headline: "Escaped Leopard Believed Spotted."

Dullest headline? Well, according to the arbiters of the *New Republic* contest, the honour goes to the editorial department of Alabama's *Huntsville Courier,* which ran a story under this flag: "Local Woman, 82, Cleans Out Desk."

Personally, I can think of a half-dozen stories that bubble up from six poignant words like that.

But then, I don't write headlines for a living.

Many Thanks, Julia

Thank you.

Now there's another phrase I wish I heard less often.

Not because I'm against gratitude — I'm not. It's just that we use the phrase too loosely. It doesn't mean much any more.

"Many thanks!" I burble to the sales clerk who hands me a fistful of nickels and dimes. "Thanks a lot!" I crow to the bus driver I will never see again as I hop out the front door of the Greyhound. "Thanks for everything!" I hoot at telephone voices, receptionists, and other sundry passing strangers whose lives touch mine with the slightest of gossamer jiggles.

I'm not saying that these people don't deserve to be thanked — only that it leaves me with nothing to say when I come up against something for which I am truly grateful.

Like my health. My family. My friends. I mean, Jake's a great buddy, but if I ever went up to him and said, "Hey, Jake — many thanks for being my friend, eh?" he'd probably wrestle me to the ground and take away my car keys.

As a rule, women handle this sort of thing much better than we strutting, grunting, sensitivity-deficient studs. With most men, it's just "Hey, how about them Maple Leafs?" Women, on the other hand, have a thousand ways of saying thank you with their eyes, their hugs, their phone calls, and their random notes.

What got me ruminating on this gratitude kick was an item I spied in the paper. The story concerns Julia Sommers, a struggling single mother who puts in fourteen-hour days as a waitress and a motel maid to put food on the table and clothes on the backs of her two little kids.

Well, Julia's luck changed recently. She was crossing a shopping

51

mall parking lot when she spotted, among the Dixie cups and the beer cans and the leaves, a necklace. A very beautiful necklace.

She took it to a jeweller and asked for an appraisal. The jeweller sighed, screwed his jeweller's loupe into his eye, squinted, stiffened, then reverently handed the necklace back to the woman.

"Off the top of my head," he told Julia Sommers, "approximately two hundred thousand dollars."

So Julia's on easy street, right? And she's going to cash in the choker and quit her two jobs and move somewhere nice and quiet and spend the rest of her life being grateful to Lady Luck for making her cross that shopping mall parking lot, right?

Wrong. That's you and me. What Julia did was dig into her handbag and fork out about fifty dollars to pay for newspaper ads. The ads read "Found: one necklace in the Four Way Shopping Mall Plaza. Owner call and describe." And Julia's telephone number was printed below.

It wasn't long before Julia's phone rang and a woman's voice — quavering with gratitude — described how she'd lost the necklace while shopping. She was a banker's wife and she described the necklace perfectly. Julia agreed to meet her. At the mall, because, well, Julia wasn't all that proud of the apartment building she had to live in.

At the mall, Julia saw a woman climb out of a car — a Rolls-Royce — and hurry towards her. She identified herself as the banker's wife and took the necklace from Julia with trembling hands. She thanked Julia profusely, gushing that words couldn't express how much it meant to have it back.

And then, pulling a wad of bills out of her handbag, she said, "And Julia, your honesty should not go unrewarded."

And the banker's wife handed Julia two dollars, thanked her again, and drove away.

Leaving Julia Sommers forty-eight bucks in the red for those classifieds, and very sorry that she didn't pawn the rocks, right?

Wrong again. "I never thought about keeping it, even after the jeweller told me what it was worth," she says. "I teach my daughters to be honest, and I'm no hypocrite."

That you aren't, ma'am. But you are a lady with a lot of class — something the "lady" in the Rolls-Royce with the diamonds and emeralds winking out of her neck wattles will never be.

And for that, Julia Sommers, I say thank you. And I mean it.

Famous Last Words

There was a story in the *Globe and Mail* recently about a parish council in Shrivenham, Oxfordshire, England, that's taken to censoring epitaphs that appear on tombstones in its cemetery. The council has declared "inappropriate" the chiselled legend on the tombstone of one Keith Woodward. Mr. Woodward's tablet reads "I Told Them I Was Ill." The parish council finds such a sentiment just a shade too flip for its hallowed boneyard.

A pity the councillors worried about *tone*. They could have had Mr. Woodward on plagiarism. His epitaph is one that the Irish wit Spike Milligan invented and claimed for his own decades ago, back when clever epitaphs were all the rage. The American writer George S. Kaufman wanted the phrase "Over My Dead Body" to appear on his earthly marker. Dorothy Parker opted for "Excuse My Dust."

It's not necessary to be famous to have a clever epitaph. A cemetery in Ruidoso, New Mexico, contains the final resting place of one Yeast, Jonathan. His tombstone reads: "Here Lies Johnny Yeast. Pardon Me for Not Rising."

And rumour has it there's a tombstone in Thurmond, Maryland, that reads: "Here Lies an Atheist. All Dressed Up . . . Nowhere to Go."

Of course, it's a relatively simple thing to whittle away a few of your waning hours carefully handcrafting some clever exit line. The real trick is to come up with something pithy when the Grim Reaper bushwhacks you without warning. That's when you get slightly loopier lifetime summations such as King George V's "Bugger Bognor!"; or Tallulah Bankhead's throaty "Bourbon." Lady Montagu went out in a splendour of British understatement and stiff upper-lippery. Her last words were "It has all been veddy interesting."

But some are troupers to the end. When a clergyman asked a dying Henry Thoreau if he had made his peace with God, Thoreau replied, "I was not aware we had quarrelled." And the playwright Brendan Behan, bless his irreverent Irish heart, whispered to the nun who was holding a damp cloth to his forehead, "Bless you, sister. May all your sons be bishops."

And I would have liked to have known George Appell better — although it might have been dangerous for my health. Mr. Appell was a crook and a murderer who went to his death in the electric chair in Chicago about half a century ago. But not before he turned to the chaplain, the reporters, the witnesses, and the police guards and wise-cracked, "Well, ladies and gentlemen . . . you're about to see a baked Appell."

My favourite last words? A self-generated epitaph that's neither flippant nor solemn, more . . . just right. It came from the lips of Thomas Stonewall Jackson, the Confederate general who, on his deathbed in 1863, turned his gaze to a friend and said: "Let's go over the river . . . and sit in the shade of the trees."

And that, it seems to me, is just about the perfect way to turn out the lights.

How's That Again?

Spent a day down in Canada's southernmost city last week: Windsor, Ontario. Windsor's a great city, with a fairly substantial francophone population — but you'd never guess it from the way Windsorites fracture French. There's an island in the Detroit River, just off Windsor, called Ile de Peche — Island of Fish. Except it isn't called that. The folks in Windsor call it Peach Island. There's a street downtown that bears the fine old French name of Pellissier. But don't ask for it. What you want to ask for is Pel-*Ish*-er Street. And how about the name of Canada's most famous prime minister of recent years? You wouldn't think anybody could much mangle the fairly simple name Pierre, would you? There's a Pierre Street in Windsor. It's pronounced Peerie.

Well, if you're going to mispronounce place names, Canada is the country to do it in. We've got the city of To-ron-to, but only Americans call it that. To the rest of us, it's Tronna. And we have — last time I looked — the province of Kwabec or Kwebec or Kaybec, depending on how you roll your consonants. And as Alan Rayburn points out in his book *Naming Canada,* there is Dal-HOW-see University in Halifax, Dal-HOO-see Street in Ottawa, and a Port Da-LOO-see down near Niagara Falls. There is also GREEN-ich, Nova Scotia; GREEN-wich, New Brunswick; and GREN-ich, Prince Edward Island. That's what they sound like. They are all spelled G-R-E-E-N-W-I-C-H.

When I lived in Thunder Bay, we could always spot an outsider by the way he or she pronounced the town or the lake spelled N-I-P-I-G-O-N.

It's *Nip*igon. Greenhorns always said Nipi-GAWN or, more rarely, Nipeejun.

Funny how we put our linguistic stamp on places — places we

don't even live in or speak the prevailing language of, necessarily. Why do we say Paris instead of Paree, as the inhabitants do? Would it be so hard to say Roma instead of Rome? The Spanish city is Se*villa*, not Seville or SEV-ille.

In the state of Minnesota, there's a town with the quintessentially Spanish name of Montevideo.

Except Minnesotans refer to it as Monty Video.

Which reminds me of one of my favourite scrambled place-name stories. A brash New Yorker arrives at a restaurant in a small town in Texas . . . a town's name spelled M-E-X-I-A. How do you pronounce that?

Mecksia?

Mek-SEE-ya?

Me-hee-a?

Ma-high-ya?

Well, this is a take-charge guy, this New Yorker. You wanna find out something, ya ask, am I right? He buttonholes a busy waitress. Puts his face close to hers and says, "Listen, sweetheart, I want ya to say the name of this place for me very slowly and very clearly, you got that?"

The waitress looks at the guy, says okay, puts her hands on her hips, and roars, "MMMMMMMmmmmmmmmc-Donnnnnnnn-alllds."

The Smallest Room in the House

Let's talk toilets.

Of course, we hardly ever call them toilets, do we? We speak of latrines and lavatories, of loos and johns and jakes and . . . Well, then we go really wimpy. We refer to stations, the little boy's room — and rest rooms.

You know anybody who ever went to a rest room to rest?

This is not just a case of North American fuddy-duddiness. The French murmur about wishing to visit *la salle d'eau* — literally, the room of water. In Spain you ask for the *retrete* — or the *dobleay vay cay* — which is a direct cop from the British WC, standing for "water closet."

Water closet? Gimme a break. If the toilet's a water closet, what does that make my artesian well?

'Twas ever thus, apparently. Humankind has long been masking the earthy realities of the room with the toilet in it in euphemisms softer than five-ply Delsey. Ancient Israelites referred to the backhouse as the House of Honour. Venerable Egyptians called it the House of the Morn. Come to think of it, my old man used to call it the Throne.

The irony is, the word we're all avoiding when we priss on about the john, the loo, or the little room — to wit, "toilet" — is a euphemism itself. It comes from the French *toilette,* which is derived from a word meaning cloth or woven material. That's where our word "toiletries" comes from, not to mention "toilet water" — which, of course, is not what logic would lead you to believe.

Which leads me to my favourite rest-room review retort. It concerns a certain playwright whose production was panned mercilessly by a newspaper critic. With icy calm, the playwright folded up the review neatly, tucked it under his arm, and retired to his . . . comfort station.

There, he jotted a note to the hostile reviewer.

"Sir," it read, "I am seated in the smallest room of the house with your review before me. Shortly, it will be behind me. Sincerely, et cetera."

And let's make that the bottom line on toilets.

Bless You!

You want to know how it starts? I'll tell you how it starts. First, you take a deep breath, then you close off your glottis. That's the little thingamabob in your throat near the top of your windpipe. What happens when you do that is you shut down the larynx, which in turn creates pressure on your lungs. When the pressure builds up to the max, suddenly your glottis pops open, and and and AND AND . . .

You sneeze.

You sneeze. I sneeze. Everybody sneezes. It's something we all have in common, right around the world. If you sneeze among English speakers, somebody says, "God bless you." German sneezers get a "*Gesundheit*." Russians exclaim, "*Bud zdorov*"; Arabs say, "*Yarhama Kum Allah*"; the Chinese say, "*Bai sui.*" The ancient Romans were more formal. When Caesar sneezed, his consuls cried, "Jupiter preserve you!"

Except they said it in Latin.

It all means pretty much the same thing. The non-sneezers are invoking the gods to protect the sneezer from invasion by an evil spirit. The ancients believed that demons would take advantage of the sneezer's temporary discombobulation to scuttle down his throat and set up housekeeping. They also believed that a quick pious oath could cross-check the goblin in mid-scuttle.

Interesting phenomenon, the sneeze. Next time you indulge, you better hope there's no cop with a radar gun around. The air that comes out of your nose fires out particles of nasty bits at speeds that can reach one hundred miles an hour.

Tell you another thing about sneezing: you cannot keep your eyes open when you do it. Nobody seems to know exactly why that is, but it can be a hazard for the serial sneezer. The person who sneezes several times in succession. Like my sister. Most people call her Ruth, but in family gatherings she's known as Ahoo Ahoo Ahoo Ahoo Ahoo.

Lucky for my sister she doesn't live in South America. Latin Americans have a wee tradition they lay on multiple sneezers. After the first sneeze they say, "Jesus." Sneeze again and they cry, "Maria!" On the third sneeze they shout, "Jose" — but if there is no third sneeze, they cluck and say, "*Jose se quedo en la carpinteria*" — Joseph stayed in the carpenter's shop.

I'm not sure the Spanish language contains enough responses to handle my sister when she goes on a sneeze binge. I'm sure they'd have trouble with an English woman by the name of Donna Griffiths. Donna started sneezing — an average of twenty times a day — in January 1981. She didn't stop sneezing until 1983 — racking up 978 straight days of sneezing.

Not much fun — but it did get her into *The Guinness Book of Records*. And — if there's a Jupiter in heaven — a free lifetime supply of Kleenex.

English as a Second Language

$\mathbf{B}$ack in the eighteenth century there was an Englishman by the name of Benjamin Schulze who could recite the Lord's Prayer in 215 languages. A certain Cardinal Mezzofante of Bologna was apparently fluent in "some fifty or sixty" tongues. Mr. Berlitz — the guy who invented the Berlitz method — claimed fluency in fifty-eight languages . . . and Sir John Bowring, one-time governor of Hong Kong, claimed to speak one hundred languages and to read one hundred more.

Even the American wit Dorothy Parker had a lady friend whom she said "speaks eighteen languages and can't say 'no' in any of them."

My question is, with all these lingomeisters around — how do you account for foreign-language movie subtitles? You know — the line of English translation that runs along the bottom of the screen while Bruce Lee or Toshiro Mufine is rattling away in Chinese or Japanese? They don't always quite . . . capture the nuances, do they?

Here's a few collectible English subtitles culled from films made in Hong Kong over the past few years:

"You daring, lousy guy!"

And another one shouted by a policeman at a crook who's barricaded himself in a house: "I'll fire aimlessly if you don't come out!"

There's a Chinese movie where the hero is about to be executed by a firing squad. His last words? "I am damn unsatisfied to be killed in this way."

And my favourite. The muscle guy from the Triad looks at the hero and growls menacingly: "Take my advice or I'll spank you without pants!"

Ah, well, there was a fine old tradition of mutilating cinema English long before the Easterners gave us their two-yen worth. The movie mogul Sam Goldwyn was legendary for twisting simple speech into hilarious linguistic pretzels at the drop of a misplaced metaphor. He repeatedly referred to Joel McCrea, one of the stars in his stable, as Joe McRail. And once Goldwyn showed off the latest addition to his art collection — a canvas he introduced proudly as "my favourite Toujours Lautrec."

Sam was not a linguist. He had enough trouble handling English. Once he toyed with the idea of buying the rights to a novel that dealt with alternative sexuality — not what you'd call commercially viable subject matter in Hollywood of the 1940s and 1950s. A studio adviser whispered in his ear, "Sir, we can't film that. It's about lesbians."

"All right," said Goldwyn, "where they got lesbians, we'll use Austrians."

But the Naugahyde mantle for garbled cinematic English must, I think, go to the film director Michael Curtiz. Curtiz directed many movies, including the classic *Casablanca*. Curtiz — a.k.a. the Mad Hungarian — had a wonderful sense of mastery on the movie set, but less when it came to the English tongue. It was Curtiz who, during the filming of *The Charge of the Light Brigade,* attempted to initiate the stampede of hundreds of riderless horses past the cameras by booming through his megaphone "Hokay, now . . . brrang on de ampty horses!"

The entire set collapsed in laughter, which sent the Hungarian-born Curtiz into a towering rage. "YOU AND YOUR STINKING EENGLISH LANGUAGE!" he boomed through the megaphone, "YOU THEENK I KNOW BUGGER NOTHING. BUT I AM TELLING YOU, I KNOW BUGGER ALL!"

Cock-Eyed Cockneys

One of the enduring marvels of the English language for me is cockney. Specifically, cockney rhyming slang. Nobody knows exactly how cockney rhyming slang originated, but it's at least a century and a half old and shows no sign of withering up and blowing away. It's a kind of secret language used by people living in a specific area of London. In cockney rhyming slang, objects are identified by other objects they rhyme with. Thus "trouble and strife" is cockney slang for "wife." "Apples and pears" means "stairs." A cockney will talk about his "china" when he means his buddy. It comes from "china plate," which rhymes with "mate." A cockney might ask you to open the "burnt cinder." He's talking about the window. Or "winder." And Elephant and Castle, a cockney stronghold in London, comes from, believe it or not, Spanish — *infanta de Castile.* "Cor, that's yer Elephant and Castle, innit?"

Is cockney dying? Not by a long shot. There's a new cockney dictionary out on the stands right now that shows just how lively — and adaptable — cockney is.

Captain Kirk is being immortalized in the streets of London. "Captain Kirk" is what the cockneys say when they mean "work." Cockney car dealers refer to money as "Arthur Ashe" — as in "cash" — while other cockneys talk of "Bugs Bunny" — rhymes with "money." Cockneys prefer to wash their faces with a bar of Bob Hope. And — get this, Canucks — when they want to clean up a mess on the floor, cockneys haul out the Vancouver. Which is rhyming slang for Hoover.

David Bowie will be remembered by cockneys long after his records and CDs have turned to dust in the remainders bin. "David Bowie" rhymes with "blowy" . . . and that's why cockneys refer to hurricanes as "David Bowies." Speaking of blowing, this new dictionary finally answers a question I've long wondered about. Why do we speak of jeering as "blowing a raspberry"?

Well, to get that, you have to understand that it comes from a longer bit of cockney slang. The full phrase was "blowing a raspberry tart."

There. I hope we've cleared the air on that one.

Hi! My Name Is . . .

I don't know how today is shaping up for you, but it's already a red-letter one for me. Red letter because I have a brand new discovery to add to my Lifetime List.

Spotted it as I was reading my *Manchester Guardian* this morning at breakfast. It was in a letter to the editor. A solemn and sonorous letter about . . . I forget what it was about. Doesn't matter. Point is, the letter concluded "Yours sincerely . . ." and it was signed "Ms. Primrose Peacock, Taunton, Somerset."

Ha! Primrose Peacock! A definite keeper! It goes on my Lifetime List of Oddball Names. Right up there with Mrs. Verbal Funderburk of Lakeland, Florida; Mr. Humperdinck Fangboner, an Ohio timber merchant; and one Zoltan Ovary, a New York City doctor. Gynecologist, fittingly enough.

I used to think that baseball players had the best weird names — and there have been some good ones around the diamond — Creepy Crespi, Bingo Binks, Cannonball Titcomb, and Pickles Dilhoeffer.

But other sports are equally rich in loopy monikers. Didn't hockey give us Sheldon Kanegeiser? (A defenceman whose name was longer than his NHL career.) And who can forget the great New York Giants quarterback Y.A. Tittle? The initials by the way stand for Yelberton Abraham. Not hard to see why he went with Y.A.

But odd names are not solely a sports phenomenon. Entertainers often inflict nomenclatural weirdness on their offspring. David Bowie called his kid Zowie. Zowie Bowie. Frank Zappa made sure his children would make it to the List of Weirds on more than the strength of their surname. He dubbed his children Moon Unit and Dweezil.

Names . . . did you know that this year alone more than 20,000 residents of Ontario are registering a name change? Many of them just don't want to hear themselves addressed by the names their parents inflicted on them. That would include people like Magdalena Babblejack, Sibble Bibble Berp, Skidmore Mouseyfoot, and Yankee Doodle Dangle Wang.

And no, I did not make any of those names up. Actual living persons have driver's licences with those names on them. If you don't believe me, ask the keeper of records at Morris Harvey College in Charleston, West Virginia. Go ahead . . . phone him up. Ask for Mr. Hogjaw Twaddle — there's only one on campus.

Names . . . they can be great fun. And they can drive you nuts. There's a story about Richard Nixon in one of his non-Oval Office incarnations, signing copies of his autobiography, *Six Crises,* at a bookstore. A customer handed Nixon his copy for autographing. Nixon asked, "To what name shall I address the inscription?"

The customer smiled and said, "Mr. Nixon, you've just met your seventh crisis. My name is Stanislaus P. Wojeshlevskowowski."

A Spooner in the Works

What is with this world, I ask ya? We can find the time to honour St. Valentine and St. Patrick; we set aside a week in reverence to Kidney Awareness, National Soil Conservation — even a Shoe Week. My events calendar has room for a Bob Marley Day, a Wear a Sun Hat Day, even an International No Diet Day.

But not a month or a week or a day or a moment has been dedicated to the memory of a comedic genius born a century and a half ago. To wit — or rather woo tit — the Reverend William Archibald Spooner.

The Reverend Spooner belongs to the school of unconscious comedy. Which is to say, he was funny without meaning to be. As well as being an Oxford scholar, Reverend Spooner was a carrier of the affliction known as "metathesis." It means to transpose words. To turn expressions around . . . to say mings you don't thean.

If you dollow my frift.

Except that the Reverend Spooner took metathesis to undreamed of heights. Thus in a sermon he once intoned, "Our Lord . . . is a shoving leopard." Another time, he announced that the title of the next hymn to be sung was "Kinqering Kongs Their Titles Take."

Reverend Spooner was not just a scholar and an ecclesiastic — he was a patriot too. Once, he addressed the prospect of welcoming returning soldiers with this promise: "When the boys come home, we shall have all the hags flung out." A bit of a two-wheel fitness freak too. "For pure enjoyment," said Spooner, "give me a well-boiled icicle every time."

Spooner's tongue was a two-headed serpent. It made him say "scoop of boy trouts" when he meant "troop of boy scouts";

he informed a nervous bridegroom that it was "kisstomary to cuss the bride." And on one occasion announced to a parishioner, "Mardon me, Padam, this pie is occupewed. Allow me to sew you to another sheet."

Mind you, he could be a stern taskmaster when the situation called for it. One time, Spooner confronted a balky student with the accusation: "Johnson, you hissed my mystery lecture. In fact, you have deliberately tasted two worms and can leave Oxford by the town drain!"

Lucky for the reverend that he was revered. He once raised a glass of sherry to Queen Victoria, proclaiming, "Three cheers for our queer old dean."

Well, it's a century and a half overdue, but I say let us clank coffee mugs in memory of the Reverend William Archibald Spooner — the unsung father of the spoonerism.

Well done, sir. And I feel confident that I speak for each and every member of the audio radiance on this, the Canadian Broadcorping Castration.

On the Fly

Wh`W`hat would you reckon are the three most paralyzing words you can say to a guy?

Stick 'em up?

The rabbit died?

Revenue Canada calling?

I submit these three words: *Your fly's open!*

Hard to say why a guy will look so . . . stricken when he hears those three little words. I mean, it's not the end of the world. It's not like they're telling you your feet are on backwards or you're bleeding from the ears. We're talking about a simple costume adjustment here . . . and yet the way we guys react, you'd think we'd just been told there was a sniper on the premises.

Seems to be a fairly universal reaction too. There are a host of euphemisms available to break the news gently. I remember looking puzzled when a teacher informed me my flag was flying at half-mast until the giggles of my more worldly colleagues tipped me off. In some parts of the world they tell the hapless male that "It's one o'clock at the waterworks," or "Gazelles are in the garden." Also somewhat inexplicably, some whistle blowers will tell the undone male, "Your nose is bleeding," or "There's a star in the east."

In New Guinea there's a pidgin phrase you can't help loving. Neglect to properly adjust your vestments coming out of a privy in Papua and a native is likely to murmur:

"Maket i op."

That means "The market is open."

I think my all-time favourite, however, is a musical warning I learned about from a fellow in Sackville, New Brunswick. It's a whistled tune —

the famous "Song of the South." The one with the lyrics that go: "Zipper dee doo dahhhhhh . . ."

Lots of different ways to tell a guy he's making a fashion statement he probably wishes he wasn't — but how to recover? What's a guy to do? The spastic pirouette followed by a two-handed, cross-legged clutch? That's less than suave.

Personally, I've always dreamed of handling it with the aplomb shown by Winston Churchill. Once, coming out of the washroom in the British House of Commons, Churchill was approached by an MP, who whispered that his clothes were — ahhhhh — somewhat disarranged, if he caught the man's meaning.

The great man, then in his eighties, looked at the MP and growled, "What of it? Dead birds don't fall out of nests."

Oh, My Head

Consider the word "hang."

Sounds Chinese, doesn't it? Hang. Not, though. It's a venerable English verb — and one of the hardest working words in the language.

A person can hang in or hang out. You can hang around or about. You can hang loose, or you can hang tough. You can hang fire; you can hang on for dear life. You can hang back, hang-glide, hang out your shingle, hang five, or you can hang a moon. It's possible to be hung *out* to dry, *like* a horse, or *by* the neck until dead — possibly the ultimate hang-up.

Personally, I wouldn't mind being hanged by the neck until dead. Right now. That's because last night I took the opportunity to really hang one on. Which left me with this hangover.

Office party. Occupational hazard this time of year. I mean, consider the premise. By saying, "Office party? Terrific! Yeah, I'll be there," you are agreeing to voluntarily put yourself in a confined space with people you have to see every working day, some of whom sign your cheques . . . and you are then going to wash down weaselly little morsels of pseudo-food with copious glasses of a mind-altering drug. Aside from committing a kamikaze career move, you are willingly agreeing to stay up all night in crowded quarters eating and drinking everything in sight.

That is the modus operandi of a cockroach.

And then there's the Post-Mortem. The Afterlife of the Party. For me, office parties almost always include a morning-after soliloquy to my bathroom mirror. As I examine the wreckage through eyes that look like raisins in two bowls of rhubarb, my mouth is mumbling things like: "Oh, God. Oh, Lord. Aw, I didn't say that. I couldn't have said that. Oh, Lord."

I don't think I was . . . *too bad* at the office party last night. But that's the maddening thing, isn't it? You're never quite sure. And daylight has a way of changing perceptions. What seemed like scintillating wit at the height of festivities can look embarrassingly moronic by dawn's early light.

Hangover. Sounds almost gentle, doesn't it? Sure doesn't sound as grim as it feels. Sort of like being seasick without getting the ocean view.

I'll say one thing for the hangover, though: it kind of takes your mind off remorse. Samuel Johnson said that if a man knows he is to be *hanged* in a fortnight, it concentrates his mind wonderfully. A hang-*over* is a bit like that. There's no room in your throbbing skull for re-runs of last night's debacle. That pompous, pencil-necked clown in accounts receivable — did I really call him a pompous, pencil-necked clown? Over the PA system?

Perhaps the station manager failed to appreciate my spontaneous karaoke rendition of "Everybody Must Get Stoned," complete with air guitar.

And how come the left sleeve of my sports jacket looks like it's been steeped in a vat of tamari sauce?

Important questions all. But for another day. I'm going to hang up my computer mouse in a moment. Then I'm going to hang a left out of the office and head back to my place. I plan to hang a Do Not Disturb sign on the door, and just kind of hang out for the afternoon with the lights off and a damp cloth hanging off my dome. And if anybody calls — even the pompous, pencil-necked clown from accounts receivable — I'll hang up in his ear. I will not be taking calls. Or making them. Not today. Maybe tomorrow.

As Scarlett liked to say, "Tomorrow is another day."

And to paraphrase Rhett Butler, "Frankly, right now, I don't give a hang."

Team Spurts

George Bernard Shaw once squinted down his nose at an unfolding soccer match and sniffed: "Games are for people who can neither read nor think." Pretty harsh, even for a curmudgeon like Shaw — but the more I see of professional sport, the more I suspect the old Irish grump might have deserved that free kick.

For the past year or so, I've been watching the progressive deification of basketball. For most of my life (and if you grew up in Canada, for most of yours), basketball was a game you played in high-school gym class, or in somebody's driveway whose old man was well-heeled enough to afford paving. And that was pretty well it for basketball in Canada. There were no pro-basketball leagues that I ever heard of. . . . There were no travelling teams of human giraffes bussing in from Hamilton or Kamloops or Antigonish to play a weekend double header. The only pro team I ever saw play in Canada, man and boy, was the Harlem Globetrotters on one of their infrequent round-the-world tours. And the Globetrotters didn't play basketball; they played *with* the basketball. The game of basketball is to the Globetrotters what Greco-Roman wrestling is to Randy "Macho Man" Savage.

Then, all of a sudden, somebody told the National Basketball Association that there were unplucked wallets north of the border. Bingo. Vancouver and Toronto get NBA franchises, and the fans, with instant Pavlovian devotion, materialize out of the ether and start beating down the doors.

Now, you pick up a newspaper, turn on a radio, and you get wall-to-wall glowing reports of the latest exploits of Michael Jordan, Hakeem Olajuwan, and Bryant "Big Country" Reeves.

Well, who knows? Maybe it's a gene thing. Perhaps we Canucks had

73

to sling curling stones across frozen lakes and slap hockey pucks off the boards for 130-odd years until we evolved a basketball chromosome that would allow us to appreciate a pastime that involves . . . putting balls . . . into baskets.

Whatever. There is no question that basketball has come to Canada in a mega-marketing way, along with its own Milky Way of — if not gods, then certainly royalty. Check the nicknames: Sir Charles Barkley, His Airness Michael Jordan. Not to mention Air attendants like "Magic" Johnson and Kareem "the Dream."

Doesn't address the original G.B. Shaw contention, though. Games are for people who can neither read nor think, he said. Any truth to that?

Well, let's at least give equal time to some folks who should know — guys who got to stand at the plate, or in the ring, or behind the buttocks of the offensive centre.

Yogi Berra, baseball great: "You can't think and hit at the same time."

Marvelous Marvin Hagler, boxer: "If they cut my bald head open, they will find one big boxing glove. That's all I am. I live it."

And finally, Joe Theisman, football quarterback. "Nobody in football should be called a genius. A genius is someone like Norman Einstein."

Case closed.

PART 3

Oh,
Puh-leeeeeeze!

Be Kind to Rats

I hate to flog a dead horse, but this one still has some life in it. It's hitched to a bandwagon called Political Correctness.

You know Political Correctness. That's where other people tell you what it's okay for you to think or say or do.

It is Not Politically Correct for instance, to speak, as the author of *Snow White* did, of the Three Ugly Step-Sisters.

To be Politically Correct, they are to be referred to as the Three Cosmetically Challenged Step-Sisters.

I'm not making this up. A New York high school recently cancelled a production of *Peter Pan* because some references — "redskin," "squaw," et cetera — were offensive to Native Americans.

In *New York?*

Similarly, Golden Books, the largest publisher of fairy tales on this continent, has created a non-violent version of that classic fairy tale *The Three Little Pigs*.

In the Golden Books rewrite, the wolf, instead of falling into a pot of boiling water, sleeps outside, exhausted from huffing and puffing, and the pigs build a jail around him.

After all, the wolf is an endangered species, you know.

The PC madness is everywhere. Two-thirds of British children's authors report that they have been censored on the grounds of Political Incorrectness. One author was asked by his publisher to remove a scene involving a grassy lawn on the grounds that many children do not have gardens.

In Iowa last fall, students were advised not to wear certain costumes for trick-or-treating on Halloween. Gypsy, Native American princess, African, witch, elderly person, disabled person, East Indian, and hobo were specifically to be avoided, for fear of offending the groups therein depicted.

Which leaves — what? Pumpkin costumes? Only until the Society for the Empowerment of Large Orange Vegetables forms a protest group.

Toronto has, of course, jumped on the Politically Correct bandwagon. A while back, city council voted to change the wording to "O Canada."

For the sixteenth (count 'em) time.

Henceforth, when somebody warbles "O Canada" before a Blue Jay home game, the words will not be "Our home and native land" but "Our home and *cherished* land."

"True patriot love in all thy sons command" will become "True patriot love in all of *us* command."

Seems some of the Toronto councillors found the song lyrics confusing. "I came to this country in 1966, and I've had to pretend I was a man and a native," groused Councillor Ila Bossons.

Poor thing. I trust she wears a name tag and her mother still pins her mittens to her coat sleeves.

It's worse than that. Let me introduce you to Frank Balun. Frank's a sixty-nine-year-old grandfather who's retired and likes to work in his backyard garden down in Hillside, New Jersey. One day Frank discovered that a rat was eating his tomatoes. He did the sensible thing: he trapped it in a squirrel cage, killed it with a broomstick, then called the Humane Society to come and take the carcass away.

The animal control officer responded by smacking Frank with two summons, as well as the threat of a six-month jail term and/or a fine of up to $1,500.

Frank Balun was accused of "animal abuse." The officer maintained that the rat "deserved a humane method of euthanasia."

Fortunately, they're not all loony down in Hillside, New Jersey. The public flocked to Mr. Balun's defence. The head of the local health board said he deserved a medal, not a trial. "We encourage people to kill rats because they carry disease," he said.

The charges were dropped, but Frank Balun's still steamed. "I want to have my day in court," he says. "I want people to know that this man [the animal control official] abuses authority and should be curbed."

Amen, Mr. Balun. I hope you get your chance to haul this meddling pea-brain in front of a judge.

What's more, I hope the judge clobbers the rat.

Farley Mowat: Dreamspeaker

A few years ago, an issue of *Saturday Night* magazine featured an exposé of Farley Mowat. Cover story. The cover, in fact, was a photo of Mowat with a digitally enhanced Pinocchio-length nose. It was pretty cheesy, that cover. Worthy of *Frank,* or maybe *Mad* magazine. The article inside was . . . well, less cheesy, I guess. Sharp old Canadian Cheddar to the cover's ripe Limburger.

The gist of the article was that Farley fudged the facts about his life in the North. That he did not spend as many weeks or months in Inuit camps and around wolf dens as he claimed. Also, that he unfairly maligned government officials, and that he — my favourite charge — transferred the pain he felt from his own floundering marriage onto the plight of the starving Inuit.

To which any of the millions of people around the world who have bought and read copies of Mowat's books could only respond: "So what's your point?"

The bewhiskered dynamo who looks like a stand-in for Sneezy or Grumpy *exaggerates?* This is about the worst-kept Canadian secret since Mackenzie King's tête-à-têtes with a crystal ball. Of *course* Mowat exaggerates. He's a *writer,* for God's sake. Mowat is not a Hansard reporter and he's not a government-appointed historian. He is a teller of tales. Like Shakespeare.

What does *Saturday Night* think *Macbeth* and *Hamlet* and *King Lear* are? Documentaries?

It's an overblown conceit, this Holy Grail of objectivity that journalists often claim to cleave to. Whose objectivity? Whose truth?

The article claimed Mowat has broken a trust with his public by selling fiction as non-fiction. Here's what the Saskatchewan writer

Sharon Butala — who's written both — has to say on that subject. In her book *The Perfection of the Morning,* she writes: "There is a way in which all non-fiction is fiction. The backward search through happenstance, trivia, the flotsam and jetsam of life, to search out a pattern, themes, a meaning . . . is by its nature an imposition of order onto what was chaotic. It's an attempt to give a linearity to events, many of them psychic, which had no linearity. Which, if anything, were a spiral, or had the more hectic quality of the dream.

"What is true," writes Butala, "are thoughts, dreams, visions. What may or may not be true are the order and timing of events, the perception and linking of them."

Sharon Butala says it deepest, but Farley Mowat says it shortest. "Truth I have no trouble with. It's the facts I get mixed up."

Any storyteller knows that the first thing you've got to get from an audience is attention. Nobody better at that than Farley Mowat. He'll play the bagpipes, howl like a timber wolf, drink like a longshoreman, and make you laugh till you cry. Or vice versa. And when he's got your attention, then he will make you think. And dream. That's what I'd call Mowat if I had to sum him up in one word: a dreamspeaker.

And if *Saturday Night* thinks it can bowl over that stubby, bekilted dreamspeaker with a few cheap shots from the peanut gallery — all I can say is: "Dream on, *Saturday Night* . . . dream on."

Sanitizing Insanity

Only the tiniest fraction of mankind wants freedom. All the rest want someone to tell them they are free.

IRVING LAYTON

Irving Layton, the seed bull of Canadian poetry, wrote that many years ago. He couldn't have written it recently. The Thought Police would be all over him for using the heretical term "mankind." Only "humankind" or "personkind" or some other gonadless generality will do these days.

The second scariest thing I know about the Thought Police is that they don't wear uniforms. Not external ones, anyway. They come disguised as teachers and MPs, students and housewives, lawyers and labour leaders, right-wingers and lefties.

And they don't ask for much. Just control of your mind.

The scariest thing I know about the Thought Police is that they're attacking our writers.

In Alberta, a Tory backbencher recently called for the provincial government "not to allow literature in the education system that is intolerant of any religion, including Christianity, or demeans or profanes the name of God and Jesus Christ."

The MP thinks a good first move in his Holy War would be to ban the novel *Of Mice and Men* by John Steinbeck.

That would be the same novel that has been proclaimed an American classic, that has thrilled audiences in print and on stage, that preaches a message of tolerance and love.

MP Victor Doerkson doesn't care about any of that. All he knows is that the book "uses profane words 198 times in 118 pages."

Could be, I suppose. Mr. Doerkson is the only reader I know who's so obsessed by the dirty words that he has to count them.

It's happening elsewhere in Canada too. Recently, a group of Ottawa parents sent out flyers calling for a ban on Margaret Laurence's novel *The Diviners*. The flyers complain that the novel "depicts sex . . . and many other choice four-lettered words."

It would appear that the flyer floggers could use some remedial math lessons — "sex" is a three-lettered word — but no matter. The flyers even list specific page numbers, so people can look up the steamy passages in *The Diviners* without having to wade through the whole book.

In 1993, W.P. Kinsella had to defend himself in front of a tribunal of Mohawks who accused the award-winning author of being a racist.

Kinsella, you see, is a white guy, so how could he possibly write about life on Native reserves?

That would be as absurd as, say, some obscure English playwright from Stratford trying to write about Danish princes, Roman emperors, or Italian lovers.

Kinsella, to his credit, weathered the outrage well. In fact, he revelled in it. "I've wanted to have my books banned for years. It puts me right up there with Margaret Laurence and J.D. Salinger."

Not to mention Salman Rushdie.

Thankfully, this is Canada, not Iran, that we're talking about, so nobody's issuing death threats. Yet.

But you can't help wondering. . . . After all, a few years ago, the government of Ontario toyed with a policy of "zero tolerance of harassment and discrimination at Ontario's universities."

Zero tolerance. What does that mean? Can a history professor mention the barbarities of the Inquisition if there's a Spanish student in his class likely to take offence? Nobody's quite sure.

My hunch is that academics, being the non-boat-rockers they are, will play it safe and spoon out scholastic Pablum. And our kids will get a safe, government-approved, politically correct education free of annoying kernels like Laurence, Steinbeck, and Kinsella.

And what kind of a future English Newspeak does that mean? Future, nothing — it's here, chum.

Here's a correction that ran in a Fresno, California, newspaper recently:

"An item in Thursday's *National Digest* about the Massachusetts budget crisis made reference to new taxes that will put Massachusetts 'back in the African-American.' The item should have said 'back in the black.'"

The Devil's Music,
I Tell You!

I see the government authorities in Ontario have relented. The guardians of public decorum have changed what passes for their collective mind and decreed that a Toronto rock-and-roll band will, after all, be legally permitted to refer to itself as Dropkick Me Jesus.

Excellent news for the band members, given that that's what they've been calling themselves for the past few years. Still, it was up in the air for a while. Couple of months back the boys in the band applied to register their name and the Ontario Ministry of Consumer and Commercial Relations sniffed and said, "We think not."

Why? Because, said a ministry spokesman, the name Dropkick Me Jesus "invokes violence in a religious context."

One doesn't wish to spend a lot of time speculating on how that government spokesman spends his or her spare time, but you can be pretty sure that listening to country music isn't high on the list. Otherwise the spokesman would have known that the band's name was a cop from a 1970s C&W hit — a hymn, really — called, grandly, "Drop Kick Me, Jesus, Through the Goalposts of Life."

The spokesman also hasn't spent much time reading the recent history of musical blunders. Hasn't heard of the Barenaked Ladies, who were just another local band until Toronto City Council, in a paroxysm of political correctness, kicked them off the playbill of an official city function on the grounds that their name was sexist.

The rest of the world quite rightly laughed, and the free publicity rocket-boosted BNL into an orbit of popularity they might never have gained on their own.

I hope this isn't a trend, this vetting of band names and song titles. Because if it is, government blue stockings are in for a busy time.

Country music is a regular corn field of unconventional titles. Who can forget hurtin' songs with architectural overtones such as "Flushed from the Bathroom of Your Heart," "You Got Sawdust on the Floor of Your Heart," and "You Threw Up on the Carpet of My Love."

How about songs of matrimonial dysfunctionalism, like "She Got the Gold Mine, I Got the Shaft," and the even more pungent "I Gave Her a Ring and She Gave Me the Finger."

Songs that invoke environmental observations such as "If Today Was a Fish I'd Throw It Back In" and the immortal "Let's Get Out of the Wheat Field, Darlin', We're Goin' Against the Grain."

Why, there's even a song about the sad decline of an Upper Canada College lad who ended up on Toronto's Skid Row. It's called "He Was Bred in Upper Rosedale But He's Only a Crumb Down Here."

Good old C&W. I have it on the highest authority, by the way, that country and western will be a feature of the afterlife. It will be official background music in either heaven or hell.

Which one you think it'll be says more about you than it does about the afterlife.

Canada: Feel the Diffidence!

Americans with highest glee
Applaud the climber of the tree
Englishmen have half a mind
The tree is not the proper kind
Canadians with tiny frown
Take an axe and chop it down.

ROBIN SKELTON

O Canada. It's true, you know — this country does drag a huge psychic sea anchor behind it, slowing down its passage through the international shipping lanes. Canadians are diffident, cautious — second-guessers by nature.

Americans say, "Hell, let's go for it!"

Canadians say, "But what will the neighbours think?"

Canadianism has its good side. We don't run roughshod over other national sensibilities. It will be a long time before Canadian troops invade Grenada, subvert the government of Chile, or bomb Iran. It's not our style.

But there's a downside too. There's a draggy side effect to being Canadian. Don't take my word for it. Ask the Kinsmans.

Bob and Rita Kinsman own a very successful motel/restaurant complex in cottage country — the Muskoka district of Ontario. The Blue Heron Restaurant and Motel has seven rental units, a twenty-three-seat restaurant, a lakeside dock, and a one-bedroom apartment.

A success story — with just one tiny black fly in the ointment. The Kinsmans were approaching retirement age. They wanted to get out of the grind and enjoy themselves.

And they hit on a novel way to do that. Bob and Rita Kinsman announced that they were sponsoring a competition. Contestants had to first pony up a hundred dollars each. Then they had to write a 200-word essay explaining why they would like to take over the Blue Heron Restaurant and Motel. After all the entries were in, judges supplied by the South Muskoka Literacy Society would go over the essays and choose the grand-prize winner.

In other words, for a hundred bucks and a couple of cents worth of ballpoint ink, somebody was going to win a flourishing resort business, worth close to half a million bucks.

The Kinsmans are an adventurous couple, but they're not flat out crazy. They reserved the right to cancel the contest and refund the money if they got fewer than 4,000 entries.

It became a media sensation. The newspaper wire services picked up the story. TV crews showed up to film the Kinsmans and shoot a little footage of the sun going down from the Blue Heron dock.

The story got so much airplay that even the bureaucrats in Ottawa got wind of it.

And they proceeded to do what bureaucrats do best: they killed it stone dead.

Ottawa announced that because of the minimum entry requirement, the contest was illegal.

"The police said we could appeal," noted Rita Kinsman ruefully. "But it would have to be to the Supreme Court of Canada, and that could easily cost $100,000."

So the contest is dead. The 300 entrants who have written their essays and paid their entry fee will get their money back, and the Kinsmans will try to sell their business the conventional, Canadian way. Through a real-estate agent on the open market.

Pity. A pity that a little grassroots initiative gets stomped to death by the bean-counters in Ottawa. Reminds me of the story Derek Burney, Canada's ambassador to the U.S., used to tell about the Newfoundland fisherman carrying a pail of lobsters up from the wharf. A passer-by warned him that the lobsters could get away because there was no lid on the pail.

"Not to worry, bye," says the fisherman. "These are Canadian lobsters. Soon as one makes it to the top, the others will drag him down."

Bore Your Way to Power

Can someone please explain why political biographies are best-sellers? Who wants to shell out actual loonies to read what a politician thinks of himself?

Millions of book buyers, apparently. Richard Nixon cranked out six best-selling volumes before he shuffled off to the Big Holding Tank in the Sky. Sir Winston Churchill has been dead for three decades, but his collected thoughts still sell briskly. Even Trudeau's *Memoirs* was a best-seller in the bookstores of the nation and, for insomniacs, better than a fistful of Valium and a rap in the head with a fish billy.

Nine times out of ten political autobiographies are boring — and ten times out of ten they're liberally laced with lies.

I prefer the unplanned biographies — the snippets of revelation that politicians sometimes commit to their personal journals in the privacy of their chambers after the working day of false smiles and phony hand-shakes is finished. They often reveal human, almost honest, disclosures that the authors would do anything this side of initiating nuclear Armageddon to keep secret from the press and ultimately the public.

This, for instance, from the personal diary of a man who gave most of the world nightmares not so long ago: *"April 20: Was in Dacha — had borscht for lunch. Had a rest in yard, then finished reading some stuff . . . had hair washed."*

The author? Leonid Brezhnev, supreme commander of the USSR for nearly twenty years.

God knows why Brezhnev would commit such banality to paper. Even a megalomaniac couldn't imagine that anyone would ever want to read such stuff.

But Leonid was positively lyrical compared with Louis XVI of

France. On July 14, 1789, a social earthquake slammed into Paris and turned French society upside down. Eight thousand enraged citizens stormed the Bastille and liberated the government prisoners. The French Revolution, the greatest civil uprising in the history of Western Europe, had begun. King Louis XVI was in the process of becoming King Louis the Last. A femme fatale named Madame Guillotine was already pencilling his name on her dance card.

And what do we read in Louis's own handwriting in his diary for July 14, 1789?

Just one word. *Rien.*

As far as Louis was concerned, nothing happened. Just another boring day at the palace.

Then there's Richard Milhous Nixon. The thirty-seventh president of the United States didn't keep a diary. He taped himself instead, which turned out to be even more damning.

Nevertheless, he was surrounded by lackeys who did keep notes and diaries. And some of them are more revealing than anything Nixon ever recorded on cassette. Here, for instance, is a note from the files of H.R. Haldeman, Nixon's chief of staff and lead pit bull. It refers to a meeting with the president on May 12, 1971:

> The President wants a study done for his own knowledge. The baseball game on WTOP was rained out last night. CBS . . . then put on a show to fill time. Star of show — square type — named Arch. Hippy son-in-law. The show was a total glorification of homosex. Made Arch look bad — homo look good. Is this common on TV? Destruction of civilization to build homos. Made the homos as the most attractive type. Followed "Hee Haw."

But it ill behooves we Canucks to snicker at the poverty of other nations' politicians. Canada, after all, had William Lyon Mackenzie King, Canada's longest-serving prime minister and a man who had regular chats with his dog, slipped down to the seedy streets of Ottawa on dark nights to "counsel" prostitutes, and made conference calls to his dead mother through his shaving mirror.

Come to think of it, that makes old WLM a helluva lot more interesting than Brezhnev, Louis XVI, or Tricky Dick.

88

Advancing Edjucayshun

All who have meditated on the art of governing have been convinced that the fate of empires depends on the education of youth.

ARISTOTLE

I question whether we can afford to teach Mother macramé while Johnny still can't read.

FORMER CALIFORNIA GOVERNOR JERRY BROWN

There is a can before me labelled EDUCATION and I'm hesitant to take the top off.

Hesitant because I know that any remarks I write about the State of Education These Days are bound to unleash a blizzard of faxes, letters, telegrams, and interdepartmental memos denouncing me as an unlettered lout, an untutored twit, and a gormless boob who doesn't know his astrophysics from a hologram in the ground.

All true — but it's never stopped me before.

Off with its head, then. Is it just me, or are teenage kids today even blanker than we were?

I have no hard and fast empirical evidence for this — just the grim news I read in the papers from time to time.

It bothers me to read, for example, that the West German school year works out to be a full two months longer than ours. And that Japanese and Korean kids spend all day Saturday in the classroom.

Meanwhile a North American third grader will spend 900 hours this year in a classroom — and 1,170 hours watching television.

Norwegian kids can locate 150 major cities on a world map — in Grade 3. Last week, I met a Canadian high-school graduate who didn't know where Montreal was in relation to Toronto.

An American magazine recently published a compilation of college courses, including Supervised Reading (Cornell); Surfing (Peppercorn); and Choosing a Life (Northwestern).

Then there are the impressions I pick up as I travel across the country. From Comox to Kapuskasing to Come by Chance, I swear I keep running into kids whose vocabulary seems to consist primarily of one adjective (rilly), one conjunction (like), one exclamatory phrase (no way), and the present tense of the verb "to go."

Inter-teen conversations: "So, like, I go, 'Rilly'? And she goes, like, 'No way.' And I go, like, 'No, rilly?' . . ."

So who's fault is it — the kids? Nah. They don't write the curriculum. The teachers? Nope. Canuck teachers are among the most intelligent and dedicated professionals I've ever met.

So who then? Preston Manning? The Devil? Search me. I'd write it all off as old-fogey paranoia except that every once in a while somebody from the other side of the crenellated battlements of Castle Pedagogica lobs a bomb over the wall to land at my feet.

Such as this missive, entitled "History of a Math Problem," which tracks the progress of modern thinking in education:

1960   A logger sells a truckload of lumber for $100. If his cost of production is 4/5 of his selling price, what is his profit?

1970   A logger sells a truckload of lumber for $100. His cost of production is 4/5 of his selling price, or, in other words, $80. What is his profit?

1980   A logger sells a truckload of lumber for $100. His cost of production is $80 and his profit is $20. Your assignment is to find and underline the number 20.

1990   By cutting down trees for MacMillan-Bloedel, a logger makes $20. If clear-cutting is stopped the logger will lose his job and will probably turn to a life of crime.
   • How do the squirrels feel about the logger losing his job?
   • Would you help the logger keep his job by letting him cut down the trees on your lawn? Your neighbour's lawn?
   • What do the birds say as a tree is being cut down?

The foregoing came to me on official (I won't say which) Board of Education letterhead. Depressing? Not a bit. If teachers can make fun of the absurdities of modern education, there's hope for us yet.

Litigational Lunacy

The law is a ass, a idiot.

CHARLES DICKENS

Is it just me, or are things actually getting *weirder* out there?

I'm talking about all the lawsuits going around. A few years ago, a guy in my neck of the woods got drunk, dove into a quarry, broke his neck — and then sued the township for damages.

And won. I thought that was about as dumb as the law could get. I was wrong.

As I speak, Black Flag, the insecticide people, have yanked a TV ad that featured the playing of "Taps" over some cartoon bug carcasses.

A veteran's group had threatened to sue.

A life-insurance ad that features a haggy old witch with green skin and a chin wart has been publicly slammed by — but of course — a witches' rights group.

Why didn't they just turn all the insurance adjusters into toads?

Litigational lunacy seems to be the soup du jour. There's a guy in Fort Worth, Texas, who's suing Weight Watchers. He contends that the weight-loss company's refusal to change the way it conducts its meetings is illegal and an infringement on his rights.

The guy bringing the suit, you see, is hard of hea — oops — aurally challenged. So he figures Weight Watchers' meetings should offer sign language as well as conventional conversation.

We're getting so lawsuit happy that just the threat of legal action can paralyze whole communities. Consider the case of Jeffrey Klein and his burglar alarm. Last month, Jeffrey left on an extended trip to the Far East. Four days into his trip, a neighbour tracked him down by telephone in Singapore.

It was the burglar alarm in his house back in Maryland. It had gone off on its own and had been jangling without a break for forty-eight hours. Would Jeffrey please grant permission to shut it off so the neighbourhood could get some sleep?

Sure, said Jeffrey, go ahead.

But nobody wanted to take on the job.

Even though Jeffrey Klein gave blanket permission for someone — *anyone* — to go into his house and shut off his alarm, nobody was willing to do it.

They were afraid of "liability."

It wasn't just the neighbours. The police refused to go in. The public utility refused to cut the power.

The burglar alarm kept ringing.

One of Klein's neighbours went to court to get an order to shut the damned thing off — but no judge would sign the order.

Meanwhile, Jeffrey Klein was burning up the telephone lines from Singapore trying to find somebody intrepid enough to go into his house and flip a wall switch. He finally convinced a police officer to do it.

It took the cop less than a minute to turn off the alarm, which by then had been shrieking for six full days.

Then there's the case of Steve Bowskill. He's a druggist in the town of Port Colborne, Ontario — a druggist who's been held up eight times in the past two years.

Late one night last winter, Bowskill was awakened once again to the sound of smashing glass. He got downstairs in time to see two junkies throwing fistfuls of narcotics into a van.

Which is when Bowskill, a marksman, raised his pistol, squinted down the barrel and fired.

Blowing out the rear tire of the delivery van.

Well, the wheels of justice, though notoriously balky, can positively hum every now and then. The powers that be wasted no time getting right to work on the Port Colborne break-in.

Steve Bowskill was charged with careless use of a firearm and unsafe storage of a gun.

As I speak, the Crown attorney in the case is doing his level best to jail a man whose biggest crime was protecting his property, and preventing — without bloodshed — a crime.

The law is a ass? You said it, Chuck.

Bureaucrats: The Nation's Peacekeepers

Let us briefly ponder the phenomenon of Bureaucracy. Interesting word, "bureaucracy." Comes from the French *bureau,* meaning desk or office, and the proletarian *cracy,* which is just an odd way of pronouncing "crazy." Thus, "office crazy." Don't laugh . . . it fits.

My favourite example of bureaucracy is a quotation from one of my favourite books: *Catch-22* by Joseph Heller. It's the first paragraph of a form letter supposedly sent to armed-service members' next of kin during World War Two. It goes: "Dear Mrs., Mr., Miss, or Mr. and Mrs. Daneeka. Words cannot express the deep personal grief I experienced when your husband, son, father or brother was killed, wounded or reported missing in action."

Oh, yeah, you say, but that's satire. *Catch-22* is a work of fiction.

Don't try to tell that to Diane Lazer of Allentown, Pennsylvania.

Actually, you'd have a tough time getting Miss, Ms., or Mrs. Lazer's attention anyway. She died a few years ago. But that did not stop a city bureaucrat from sending her a letter last year. A letter explaining why Mrs. Lazer was not entitled to benefits. Here's a portion of the letter: "Dear Mrs. Lazer: This case has been administratively closed for the following reasons: You died August 10, 1990, and have no survivors."

Pretty dumb right? There's more. Here's the second paragraph: "As provided by Article 181.99 you have the right to bring a private legal action. Such a lawsuit must be filed within 90 days. . . . For any questions regarding this matter you may call either Raymond C. Polaski or myself at . . ." and he gives the office phone number.

Bureaucracy. Balzac defined it as a giant mechanism operated by pygmies.

I think Jennifer Batten might second Balzac's motion. Ms. Batten, a Toronto secretary presently between jobs, received a pleasant surprise in her mailbox. It was a cheque from Canada's own Red Tape on the Rideau — Revenue Canada.

A government cheque. Made out to her.

For $499,742.13.

Jennifer Batten was perhaps not as surprised as you or I might be. That's because a couple of weeks earlier, she had received a similar Revenue Canada cheque for $211,173.43.

Not as surprised, and perhaps a tad more honest. Ms. Batten tried to give the money back.

She called Revenue Canada. She was put on hold. Four times. Three times the calls were transferred to another number, which never got answered. The fourth time she was just cut off.

But she finally got through. A snippy RevCan cipher told her she would have to go to a Revenue Canada office in Toronto and fill out several forms. Ms. Batten allowed as to how, since it was Revenue Canada's $700,000 blunder, perhaps Revenue Canada could spring a clerk and some cab fare to come and pick up the cheques.

The Revenue Canada robot dismissed that idea, but told Ms. Batten that she could mail the cheques back, warning, however, that she would be held responsible if those cheques went astray in the mail.

Last I heard, Jennifer Batten — unemployed — was still trying to give back nearly three-quarters of a million dollars to a clearly uninterested Revenue Canada. God bless her for her honesty. And her stubbornness. A lesser Canadian might have opened a Swiss bank account.

Personally, I think this is simply a case of poor deployment of resources. I think bureaucrats are wasted in institutions like Revenue Canada. They belong in uniform, with Canada's peacekeeping forces.

I mean, think about it: a bureaucrat is the ultimate peacekeeping weapon.

It doesn't work. And it can't be fired.

Wacky Statutes

It was the old satirist Jonathan Swift who said, "Laws are like cobwebs. They catch small flies, but let wasps and hornets break through."

Small flies, indeed. It was Swift's good fortune to live and write a couple of centuries ago. Which means he never got to see the fine mesh of twentieth-century cobweb laws. Did you know, for instance, that it is illegal for Halley's comet to fly over Yugoslavia? That mosquitoes are forbidden by law to live in Germany? That sport shirts with zipper fronts are banned in Havana? And that in São Paulo, Brazil, the law clearly states that any prisoner who arrives at his cell after ten o'clock at night will be barred from entering the prison and must spend the night outside the walls?

Just a few of the silly statutes and outrageous ordinances still on the lawbooks around the world. The problem, of course, is that judges and lawyers and such are exceedingly good at dreaming up new laws and regulations. They're a little less adept at unmaking them once they've worn out their usefulness — if they ever had any. You've gotta wonder about California, where a state law makes it technically illegal to set a mousetrap unless you hold a valid hunting licence. The California Penal Code also makes it a misdemeanour to "detain" a homing pigeon. How'd you like to explain that in a Los Angeles holding tank? "What are you in for, buddy?" "Aw, I got talking to this homing pigeon, and before I knew it, it was past curfew."

And everything is legally up to date in Kansas, where a law says, in part, "When two trains approach each other at a crossing, both shall come to a full stop and neither shall start up again until the other has gone." Must have a lot of idling trains in Kansas. . . .

Lots of social-propriety laws on the U.S. books. It's illegal to gargle

95

in public in Louisiana and to fall asleep in a bathtub in Detroit. If you're a woman in Raton, New Mexico, don't even *think* about riding down Main Street on horseback wearing a kimono. You'd be breaking the law. And organized crime might just as well make a big detour around Bexley, Ohio. They have a civil ordinance that specifically prohibits the placing of slot machines in outhouses.

Boy, those law-happy Yanks, eh? Not so fast. We've got some pretty wacky regulations on the books here in Canada, too. In Ottawa, there's an anti-noise bylaw that bans the buzzing of bees. In Halifax, the cops are on the watch for anyone who attempts to walk a tightrope over a public street. It's absolutely against the law to ride a camel on any British Columbia road. And it must be a little confusing to ride a bike in Edmonton, where the law states: "All bicycle riders must signal with the arm before making a turn," *and* "all bicycle riders must keep both hands on the handlebars at all times."

Which brings me to my favourite Canuck statute. This one came to my attention through a court case in Edmundston, New Brunswick. It seems fisheries officers patrolling the shores of Baker Lake came upon a fishing pole with no fisherman attached to it. The pole was there, the line was in the water. The owner of both was no where to be seen.

Temporarily. Pierre Nadeau, the angler in question, did eventually come through the brush adjusting his trousers and admitting that yes, that was his gear.

He was charged with abandoning his fishing line. But it's Pierre's excuse that renders the verdict problematical. Pierre Nadeau testified that he had left his fishing pole . . . to make love with his wife. Didn't cut any ice with the judge. Justice Alexandre Deschênes fined Mr. Nadeau a hundred bucks for, in effect, having sex while fishing.

Pity. I think Mr. Nadeau deserves the Order of Canada — or at least a niche in the Sports Hall of Fame — for elevating the essentially mind-numbing pastime called fishing to the status of a robust, fascinating, full-contact sport.

And I'm dying to know what bait he was using.

Do Not Use These Words!

Feeling a little . . . naughty? Ready to take a walk on the wild side? Okay, how about we share some . . . forbidden words. Hey. I'll even go first. You ready? If not, close your eyes, because here we go!

(1)   Common Sense.

(2)   Hometown.

(3)   It's the Right Thing to Do.

No, I'm not putting you on. Those words and phrases are really forbidden. They're copyrighted. "Common sense" belongs to the Kellogg Company. "Hometown" is the exclusive property of a firm called the Woodlands. "It's the Right Thing to Do" is a phrase that has been bought lock, stock, and barrel by Quaker Oats, Inc.

So what does it mean? That we can't ever use phrases like "common sense" or "hometown" or "it's the right thing to do" in simple conversation any more? Not exactly, but if you ever tried to use those phrases to advertise something you made, you'd have a raft of lawyers nibbling on your neck.

You should also not throw around the phrase "bend over" too loosely. Well, for a lot of reasons, but especially because Levi Strauss and Company has registered those two words with the U.S. Patent and Trademark Office. Similarly, the Hyatt hotel chain has a legal lock on the expression "wish you were here."

Is it just me — or is it in fact odd that corporations can put their brand on phrases and expressions that have been around a lot longer than they have?

It gets worse. Harley-Davidson has applied to Washington for more than a trademark — they want a "soundmark." They want exclusive legal rights to the *noise* their hogs make — so that no other motorcycle manufacturer can copy the roar.

If they win, it won't be the first soundmark to be registered with the Patent Office. Beneficial Finance Company beat them there. They've got the world rights to that hackneyed old slogan "At Beneficial (BOOM BOOM) You're Good for More!"

And the NBC television network has had exclusive jurisdiction over the famous TOOT TOOT TOOT peacock chimes for the past half-century.

There was another trademark story in the paper not long ago — the *Wall Street Journal* reported that O.J. Simpson has "agreed to share marketing rights" to his famous initials with the Florida Department of Citrus.

This apparently is a legal compromise worked out after the Florida agency attempted to block Simpson's bid to trademark his initials for his exclusive use.

That's how the *Wall Street Journal* reports it. That's not the way I heard it.

The way I heard it, the Florida Orange Juice Association was offering O.J. $1 million a year for the rest of his life.

Just as soon as he changes his name to Diet Pepsi Simpson.

Those Loveable Scamps, Our Bankers

As far as I'm concerned, nobody's ever improved on Stephen Leacock when it comes to describing the banking experience. "When I go into a bank," wrote Leacock, "I get rattled. The clerks rattle me. The wickets rattle me. The sight of the money rattles me. Everything rattles me."

For me, the truly rattling part is that Leacock wrote those words more than half a century ago . . . when banks featured such things as quill pens, hand-written passbooks, and a charmingly baroque attraction known as tellers — living human beings who frequently knew the customer by name and by sight.

Leacock got rattled by *those* banks? Can you imagine the Orillia Oracle walking into a bank these days? For one thing, Leacock probably *wouldn't* walk into a bank nowadays. He'd be bushwhacked by one of those automated cash machines long before he got his hand on the bank door.

Canada's most famous humorist, stabbing his forefinger to a pulp on the keyboard of a Johnny Cash or a Green Machine. Not a pretty vision. And not a funny one.

But funnier, I suspect, than the next Great Leap Forward of BankTrek, the Next Generation. Have you heard the latest wrinkle computer geeks at the Bank of Commerce have come up with?

They call it — Brave New Worldishly enough — BankWare II. It's a 3.5-inch floppy disc that allows customers to, and I'm quoting from the brochure here, "calculate the probability of approval for their loan applications, structure their entire personal budgets and devise their own mortgage-amortization charts." Unquote.

Says Susan Hoyle, a senior marketing spokesthingy of CIBC, "I think we've made banking fun."

Fun? Fun??? No, Susan. Sex is fun. President's Choice Decadent Chocolate Fudge Crackle Ice Cream is fun. Trying to place a collect obscene phone call to Preston Manning is fun. Devising one's own mortgage-amortization chart is Not Fun. Not even in Toronto.

On the bright side, not all bankers are computer crazy. Take, for instance, the banker cruising the aisles at a recent computer convention. A salesman buttonholes him, says, "Sir, our new Megadeck 3600 Hard Drive ROM-faced DOS-enhanced Infinite Variable Floppy Over and Under Multitasking Universal Lap Cum Desktop is the last word in computers. . . . Ask it anything, sir, anything at all."

The banker, bemused, types, "Where is my father?"

The computer clicks, whirrs, and the voice actuator sputters: "Your father is in Campbell River, B.C."

The banker snorts, "Last word, eh? My father died in Halifax ten years ago."

The salesman says, "Well, now, don't be too hasty. Perhaps the computer misunderstood. Try asking the question in a different way."

The banker shrugs, types, "Where is the husband of my mother?"

The computer says, "The husband of your mother has been dead ten years. Your father is in Campbell River, B.C., and just landed a twenty-three-pound salmon."

Taxing Times

I love T.S. Eliot, despite the fact that he was a sexless, pseudo-British, semi-fascist banker. I will tell you why I love T.S. Eliot. It's because when he wasn't balancing ledgers and anti-ing Semites, T.S. Eliot was writing poetry. And because somewhere in the miles and miles of verse he produced, he spun these two filaments. Number one, he wrote:

> *Let us go then, you and I*
> *When the evening is spread out against the sky*
> *Like a patient etherized upon a table.*

I can't explain why, but I love that image.

T.S. also wrote this line: "April is the cruellest month."

Now, you tell me: how could T.S. Eliot, who was not a Canadian taxpayer, know that about the month of April?

For April *is* the cruellest month, here in the Great White North. The time when we render unto Chrétien what is Chrétien's. April is income tax time. A kind of annual, upwardly spiralling nightmare. I don't know about you, but I have never made more — and kept less. I figure that if I can put in a couple of weeks of overtime, ignore my Visa bill, and knock over a 7-Eleven, I can juuuuuuuuust break even on my quarterly income tax instalment this semester.

Ah, well. Could be worse, I suppose. We could be living in Norway, where it is possible — believe it or not, folks — to actually pay *more* in taxes than you earn. Yep, Norway is a bean-counter's wet dream. . . . There it is actually possible to be charged more in government taxes than you make. You don't believe me? Check out the Norwegian shipping tycoon Hilmar Reksten, who back in 1974 was assessed at a modest 491 percent of his gross annual income.

Meanwhile, we lesser slugs soldier on as best we can. If I buy a tie to appear on "Newsworld," can I write it off? Dream on, pal. How about lunch with those boring suits from administration? Not this fiscal cycle, chum. But look on the bright side.

For every ten tales of woe, there's a success story. Like the story of Chesty Love.

Chesty — well, her real name is Cynthia Hess — is an exotic dancer down in Washington. She recently claimed $2,088 (U.S.) as a depreciation allowance. For her bust. Chesty really is — um — chesty. She takes a size 56 FF in a bra.

Implants are what we're talking about here. Hindenburg-type implants. Back in her BI (that's Before Implant) days, Chesty danced as Tonda Marie . . . and pulled down a paltry $750 a week. But once she had her flying buttresses augmented, Tonda (or Chesty) commanded an imposing $1,500 a week. The downside was imbalance. In December 1988, Chesty and her top-heavy twin 56s tottered down a striptease runway and toppled into the orchestra pit. Well, it's not funny. She ruptured an implant and couldn't work for all of fiscal 1989 — which is why she's asking for the depreciation allowance.

I don't know what double-barrelled surprises the Roman poet Virgil might have had underneath his toga, but I do know he spent — and claimed — the Roman equivalent of 100,000 twentieth-century Canadian dollars on a funeral for his . . . pet fly.

Crazy? Like *unus foxus.*

Virgil got to declare the fly's burial area "a cemetery," thereby avoiding payment of a hefty Roman land tax.

Taxes. Somebody once said taxes are the price we pay for civilized society. Hmmm.

Don't get me wrong. As a Canadian, I'm proud to pay taxes.

It's only that I think I could be just as proud for, oh, about half the money.

Man of the Decade
(Semi-Detached)

If you don't mind, I'd like to get my nomination in early for Schlemiel of the Decade.

Lotta competition this time out. This was the decade in which O.J. Simpson attempted the ultimate in pass interference, Oliver North tried to get in the Senate by the front door, and the future king of England revealed that, all things considered, he'd rather be a tampon — oh, there was competition, all right. But I think in the end, the paramount schlemiel of the 1990s has to be . . .

John . . . Wayne . . . Bobbitt.

You know the guy. The ex-Marine who duked and decked his wife, and got docked for his troubles with a kitchen knife.

In the short, shabby, and (until then) unillustrious life of John Wayne Bobbitt, that may just have been the best career move he could have made. Since then, he's been a media star — in the tinseliest sense of that word. He's been on "Geraldo," of course. He's been on a bunch of talk shows. As a matter of fact, there aren't many places John Wayne Bobbitt won't go if the money's right. A couple of years ago he even made an appearance at Detroit's Tiger Stadium for a baseball game. John was selling hot dogs. Hot dogs — geddit?

But, hey, that was penny-ante stuff. John Bobbitt's big time now. He's made a feature movie. A biography. It's called *John Wayne Bobbitt: Uncut* — uncut . . . geddit? Helping him with his on-screen Stanislavskian motivation is one platinum-tressed thespianess by the name of Tiffany Lords.

Ms. Lords and Mr. Bobbitt aren't just celluloid stars. They do live theatre too. Even played a string of strip clubs, including one in Toronto. What sort of a stage performer is John Wayne Bobbitt?

Laurence Olivier can probably rest easy in his grave. John doesn't have a lot of lines. But he does shuck his duds — just like Tiffany — sometimes right down to the nub. But not every show. He has to feel inspired. As a spokesman for Bobbitt Enterprises enthused at a press conference: "Anything is possible."

Yep, I think the existence of Bobbitt Enterprises — the media success of John Wayne Bobbitt — pretty well proves that anything is possible.

Hats off and bottoms up to John Wayne — my nominee for Schlemiel of the Decade.

Schlemiel? I'm not sure. I know it's a Yiddish word . . . and I like to think it means wiener.

If there's any justice . . . a cocktail wiener.

Fore Play

Well, here we are smack in the bloodshot eye of a Canadian winter, up to our chilblained niblicks in snow drifts. What better time to talk about . . . golf?

We *talk* about it here — they're *playing* it in California. Well, sort of playing it. Actually, there's been a bit of a disturbance at the AT&T Pro-Am Tournament at Pebble Beach.

Bill Murray, the comic? He's in the tournament, and the tour commissioner wishes he wasn't. Murray's an incorrigible clown. His on-the-greens goofiness draws one of the biggest gallery crowds at the tournament. You would think tournament officials would like that. They hate it. Last year Murray played a number of pranks — like pulling a grandmotherly spectator out of the stands at the eighteenth hole and spiriting her off into a bunker. Later, when the former vice-president Dan Quayle was putting, Murray yelled, "Hurry up!" in mock impatience. The crowd roared. The commissioners fumed. Earlier this week PGA Commissioner Dean Beman harrumphed that such behaviour was "inappropriate and detrimental." Murray's pro playing partner, Scott Simpson, has quietly suggested that the officials lighten up.

I'm with Simpson. For one thing, I don't think there's a funnier man on the planet than Bill Murray. I'd rather watch five minutes of him when he's on his game than an eternity of Sunday afternoons watching Fred Couples and Fuzzy Zoeller playing theirs.

For another thing, it sounds to me like golf is in mortal danger of taking itself seriously.

Come on, folks.

We're talking about a game in which grown adults dress up like pimps to hit a ball with a stick, chase it, find it, hit it again, chase it, find it, hit it again, until sundown or sunstroke renders the exercise impossible.

We're talking about a game in which the object is to cream the bejesus out of a tiny white pockmarked pill no bigger than a marshmallow. But to cream it as few times as possible. I don't like to brag, but I can hit a golf ball 150, 200 times in an afternoon, no problem. And they call me a duffer. Mighty Greg Norman would be lucky to hit the ball seventy times over the same eighteen holes. Yet Norman's a pro? This is perverse.

I'm trying not to be rigid about this. I like to go for long walks. Sometimes I feel the urge to smash things with sticks. I see no reason to pay for the privilege of doing both at once.

Ah, who am I kidding? If you noticed a sour tang in my whiff of grapeshot, you're right. The truth is: I just don't get it. Golf is for me as music was for George Eliot. "Music sweeps by me," wrote Eliot, "like a messenger with a message that is not for me."

Golf carries no messages for me. Once in a while, though, a punch line. You heard about the guy who came home from a golf game four hours late. His wife says, "Harry, where were you? Your dinner's ruined!" Harry says, "Martha, lay off. Poor Eugene is dead. Heart attack. He just keeled over on the seventh green."

Martha says, "Oh, Harry, I'm so sorry! That's terrible."

Harry says, "You're telling me about terrible! For the next eleven holes, it's hit the ball, drag Eugene, hit the ball, drag Eugene. . . ."

Hush, You Muskies!

What has happened to Canada's poor old Mounties? There was a time when the guy in the red-serge suit with the funny balloon pants and the hat that looks like a pizza with a falsie in it stood for everything that was staunch and brave and steadfast and honourable. The good old Mountie! They always get their man! On King! Mush, you huskies!

Then came the barn burnings in Quebec. Then came the Mickey Mouse franchise to Walt Disney Enterprises. Then came strangers wandering around 24 Sussex Drive in the middle of the night, chatting with the prime minister's wife, the Mountie security team lulled into torpor by cruller overload. Then came the PM providing his own security clearance during one of his patented Ottawa walkabout knockabouts.

What would Sergeant Preston think?

It's a thankless task, being a Mountie. I have a copy of the RCMP recruiting form. You know what it takes to be a Mountie? They want you to be a Canadian over the age of nineteen who is able to write, speak, and read in either official language. They want you to have a driver's licence. They expect you to have a clean record, good eyes, and sound health.

They also expect you to be willing to relocate anywhere in Canada, and to, as the form puts it, "remain mobile during your career."

And what is the government willing to pay this clear-eyed, sound-limbed, Rinso-clean gypsy? According to the last pay scale, $31,172 a year to start, rising, through five levels to a top salary of $50,508 per annum.

Mounties assigned to high-rent jurisdictions like Vancouver or Toronto can't afford to live on a salary like that. They're taking evening jobs as security watchmen and truck drivers to pay the bills. Perhaps that's why the government decided to rent them out to Walt Disney. Bring in a little extra cash to keep the horses in hay.

A miserly wage scale doesn't augur well for the calibre of recruit the Mounties can expect to attract. I heard of one guy who tried to join the force at the RCMP centre in Regina. He went in for his interview. The interviewer says he wants to ask him a couple of questions to test his general knowledge.

"Who is the prime minister of Canada?" asks the recruiter.

The guy is stumped! He rubs his chin, he grits his teeth — nothing. Then, in a flash, it comes him! "Uhhh, John Cretien?" he asks.

"Excellent! Excellent!" says the recruiter. "You're doing just fine. Now here's your second question. What is the capital of Canada?"

Another blank! Guy hasn't got a clue. Finally, he decides to hazard a guess. "Would it be Ottawa?" he inquires.

"Brilliant! Astounding!" says the recruiter. "You're doing extremely well! You're well above average! Now your final question is: who killed Jesus Christ?"

The guy is stumped. This time nothing at all comes to him. The recruiter tells him not to worry. To go home and think about it and come back next day with the answer.

So the guy goes home to his wife. "How did it go, darling?" she asks. "Did you get the job?"

"Ah," the guy says, "I have to go back tomorrow, but I reckon it's in the bag."

"Really?" says the wife. "Why do you say that?"

"Well," the guy says, "my first day and they've already got me working on a murder case."

Canada: Too Polite to Live?

The playwright John Gray once wrote that a Canadian never feels more like a Canadian than when he or she is travelling in the United States. I know what he means, but I also know that the feeling can wash over you elsewhere as well. For me it happened in an English gymnasium about twenty years ago. I was playing a game of pick-up basketball with a bunch of London guys and it was great. I am a lousy basketball player, but the Brits were even lousier, having seen the game only on the telly. So it was a lot of fun. We were making up our own rules and breaking a lot of the real ones as we went along.

Then two other guys showed up. Brush-cuts. Lean. Tall. Within seconds, one of them had grabbed the ball, pivoted, driven to the net, and sunk a basket, bowling over two little British guys in the process.

"Hey c'mon, you guys . . . it's only a game!" I protested.

The guy who had got the basket turned his American blue eyes on me and chanted his mantra. "Where I come from, we say, 'Go big or go home.'"

Well, the game was effectively wrecked. The rest of us didn't want to play that seriously. The Americans, after sinking a couple more baskets, got the message and left the court shaking their heads, I guess looking for some real competition.

The Americans were disgusted. The Brits were mystified. I merely felt . . . Canadian.

Little Bucky Beaver. Back in my hewer-of-wood, drawer-of-water, and don't-rock-the-boat mode.

It's a cliché, but it's true. We are, beside our American cousins, a placid, accommodating flock. The American Declaration of Independence calls for — no, *demands* — life, liberty, and the pursuit of happiness. Canadians have settled for peace, order, and good government.

Oh, we can rattle the windows and kick out the jams when we absolutely must, but we try to keep such behaviour confined to hockey arenas and Normandy beaches. More orderly that way.

A British friend of mine once asked me why Canada was even still around. "You're so polite, so self-effacing," he said, "and Americans are so acquisitive and aggressive. I don't understand why you Canucks haven't simply been absorbed."

I didn't really have an answer for him. God knows we haven't survived through wiliness. Or super-patriotism. I think I finally mumbled something about Canucks being a quietly stubborn bunch.

I may have been right. I offer as proof a transcript of a radio conversation between an American navy ship and a Canadian source that was monitored off the coast of Newfoundland last fall.

The transmission goes like this:

American ship's radio: Please divert your course 15 degrees to the north to avoid a collision.

Canadian radio: Recommend you divert *your* course 15 degrees.

American ship's radio: This is the captain of a U.S. Navy ship. I say again, divert your course.

Canadian radio: No, *I* say again, divert *your* course.

American ship's radio: This is an aircraft carrier of the U.S. Navy. We are a large warship. Divert your course *now!*

Canadian radio: This is a Canadian lighthouse. Your call.

PART 4

And Another Thing That Bugs Me . . .

PCs — Let's Put the Boots to Them

Ever get the feeling you don't quite have the horsepower to keep up on the information highway? A couple of ice ages ago I discovered I was the last kid on the block to be typing on an Olivetti manual. So I bought an electric typewriter. Which almost instantly went the way of the dinosaurs when *electronic* typewriters came along. They in turn were wiped out by personal computers, which arrived the day after I got my electronic typewriter. I bought one, of course.

It didn't stop with my first PC. I updated. I expanded. I slapped on an extra hard drive and a full-colour monitor and a modem. And a rear-view side mirror so I could keep track of what was coming up the info turnpike behind me.

Some things don't change, of course. When I want to write something I still sit down at the same old desk, still stare at the same old patch of wallpaper. Still fuss and fidget and curse and groan and bang my forehead on the keyboard until I draw blood. Ah, but when inspiration strikes *now,* I get to fire up this huge *Starship Enterprise* console and I wait while the monitor and the printer warm up and I tap in the code for the program I use and I wait some more while the photons dance across the screen.

Sometimes it's a couple or three minutes before my computer signals that it's okay to start typing. This is a lot better than the old days. With my Olivetti you just fed it a sheet of paper and you were on your way. In the deep end. A guy didn't have time to think.

I'm no computer expert, but I'm pretty sure the overall trend in computers is faster and smaller. Especially smaller.

You don't have to be Bill Gates to figure that out. Those first computers, back in the forties, occupied whole city blocks, while mine isn't much bigger than, say, the cockpit of a 727. But then, I'm already laughably obsolete. Computer owners in the know work on laptops about the size of an open book. Or even palmtops. Little gizmos you can slip in your jacket pocket.

And computers are getting even smaller. The next one is so small you can carry it in your shirt pocket . . . or even behind your ear. According to a report in the *L.A. Times,* thousands of Americans are latching on to this latest development in miniaturized word-processing. The prototype FP, it's called. Why so popular? Well, portability for starters. The entire unit consists of two parts, and together then don't even weigh half an ounce. Then there's the fact that the FP system operates on an independent power source. You don't need access to an electrical outlet, nor do you have to lug around a heavy adapter. You don't even need batteries.

But it's more than mere convenience. Converts claim that the FP units lend a subtle elegance and personal enhancement to written communication that you just can't get with conventional computers.

Nancy Andreasen is one unabashed enthusiast of the new portable communication system. She says the most distasteful aspect of her job as the editor of the *American Journal of Psychiatry* is rejecting 80 percent of the papers that are submitted for publication. When she has a rejection to compose, she eschews her desktop computer and turns to her FP system. "It conveys to them that I care," she says. "I've learned . . . that it's harder to be mad at someone who writes you a personal note."

So that's why she employs her Pelikan Toledo for the chore.

Pelikan Toledo — that's the brand name that Andreasen prefers. The generic name is FP, as I said. Or, if you want the full title, it's fountain pen.

I'd order one if I thought it wasn't just a fad.

Of course, that's what I said about computers when I had my Olivetti.

Weeding Out the Bad Guys

Genghis Khan. Adolf Hitler. Pol Pot. Lucretia Borgia. All names that will live forever in the annals of infamy and villainy.

But far from the only names that belong on the list. How about . . .

Cypress Spurge and his evil cousin Leafy?

Dodder?

Black-Seeded Proso Millet?

And the repulsively monickered Tuberous Vetchling?

Mass murderers? Serial killers? Psychopathic terrorists?

Naw. All of the above are as common as crabgrass and as near as your backyard.

My backyard, anyway. All of the aforementioned are garden-variety noxious weeds, capable of showing up in the cracks between your patio stones faster than you can say, "Quick, Martha — hand me the Killer Kane!"

And these aren't the only verdant varmints that cry out for vigilance. Alert lawn owners must also be on the lookout for perennial pests like the Poison Sisters — Ivy, Oak, and Hemlock — not to mention the ubiquitous thistle — sow, bull, Canada, nodding, Russian, and Scotch.

I don't know what it's like where you live, but we've got Weed Police in my neck of the woods. Undercover agents for the Public Works Department whose job it is to snoop down laneways and peer over garden fences to see if anybody's harbouring a clandestine crop of burdock, milkweed, or wild carrot.

Oh, well. Keeps them out of the pool hall, I guess.

The thing that most ticks me off about weeds is that they're so damned easy to grow. I'm going to spend the next couple of months nursing my vegetable garden along like a flock of premature babies.

And for what? After hours of mulching and composting and fertilizing and coddling, I will be rewarded with a crop of:

- pencil-sized carrots;
- tomatoes that resemble jade golf balls;
- potatoes so wizened they look like they came straight out of Tutankhamen's tomb;
- corn cobs that raccoons won't even eat;
- green peas the size (and hardness) of BB shot; and . . .
- WEEDS! Giant weeds! Rain forest weeds! Weeds with trunks the size of redwoods and leaves like elephant ears!

Why is it that the crops I want to grow practically cry out for an oxygen tent and intravenous feedings, while all around these anorexic little failures quack grass, plantain, and knapweed come up like telephone poles?

Weeds really do grow as if they have their own personal supply of anabolic steroids. Away back in 1879, scientists at Michigan State University put several lots of twenty common weed seeds into glass bottles and set them on a shelf.

Twenty-five years later, they dug some of them out and planted them. Over half of them bloomed like new and pumped out a whole new generation of seeds. Then the scientists put the experiment on the back Bunsen burner, as it were, and forgot about it. In 1959, somebody dug up and planted twenty of the original seeds again. Three of them produced viable seedlings — *eighty years* after they'd been taken out of circulation.

That doesn't surprise me. I've seen weeds punch right through the pavement in my driveway. All I want to know is: what's their secret? If I could grow eggplant the way I grow ragweed, I could change my name to the Jolly Green Giant and never darken the produce section of my supermarket again.

But I can't. I know that come harvest time, the vegetable rows in my garden will look like the Before picture in a Charles Atlas ad.

And the paths between the rows will look like a close-up of the Belgian Congo.

It's depressing. I need a pick-me-up. Perhaps a glass of wine.

Dandelion, of course.

116

I Think That I Shall Never See . . .

Yesterday I went down to the garden to sit under my favourite apple tree. Phoebe was already there. She was sitting under my tree on a beautiful summer day. And she was crying.

Phoebe cries a fair bit. She tends to take the problems of the world on her own frail shoulders. Then she buckles under the load.

I put my arm around her shoulders. "S'matter, Phoebe?" I asked.

"Oh," she wailed dramatically, "it's just the *overwhelmingness* of it all!"

I had to admit that Phoebe had a point. Take our environment. Take the cutting down of the rain forests, the annihilation of the whales, the depletion of the ozone layer, and carcinogens in the back bacon.

Pretty overwhelming, all right.

And that's without even mentioning Bosnia, Kosovo, the rise of the fascist right in Russia, never mind Ottawa, the GST, Lucien Bouchard, and ring around the collar.

No wonder Phoebe was feeling bummed out.

What are you going to tell somebody suffering from a case of the Cosmic Blues like that?

Well, I don't know what a professional psychiatrist or a practising social worker would advise, but I suggested to Phoebe that maybe she should try to narrow her focus a bit. Stop fretting about the state of the universe — worry about her own backyard. Don't think big, I told her — think small.

Think John Chapman. Back in the early 1800s, residents of western Pennsylvania were nonplussed to behold Mr. Chapman at the helm of a boatload of apple seeds, plying the waters of the Ohio River. He wore a burlap coffee sack as a poncho, a tin pie plate for a hat, and he told anyone who would listen that he was on a mission.

John Chapman was a slightly bent Yankee nurseryman whose self-appointed mission was to propagate apple orchards everywhere. He dedicated the rest of his life to it, roaming across the hills and valleys of the American Midwest, scattering seeds along the roadways, upon the riverbanks, and in forest clearings and meadows.

John Chapman got planted himself about 150 years ago in, appropriately enough, an orchard overlooking Fort Wayne, Indiana. He's dead, but the legacy of his mania lives on just about everywhere you look in rural North America.

If you've got an apple tree in your backyard — or an apple orchard in your community — legend has it that you can thank John Chapman for it.

Or, to call him by his more popular moniker, Johnny Appleseed.

Of course, you don't have to go that far back to find a tree-planting role model.

How about King Bhumibol?

He recently celebrated his fiftieth anniversary on the throne of Thailand. Most royal types would have sponsored parades and fancy dress balls with lots of pomp and pageantry. Not King Bhumibol.

He celebrated by planting trees.

Five hundred million of them.

Just imagine if every Canadian resolved, for just *one* day, not to whine about the national debt or the price of car insurance or turbans in Legions. Just imagine if every Canadian decided to plant a single tree instead.

That'd give us about 30 million new trees.

Not as many as Thailand, but it would be a start.

Beer for Bimbos

Have you ever stopped and thought about the average Canadian TV beer commercial?

Well, you're not supposed to. Stop and think about them, I mean. You're supposed to just develop this primeval thirst and go out and buy a lot of beer. But think about them for a moment. Don't you wish that Stephen Leacock or Will Rogers or Oscar Wilde could've seen just one TV beer commercial?

They're so dumb.

They feature guitar wizards or Newmanesque snooker players or preternaturally young and lively beach people — sinewy men and tawny women all lean and taut and eminently mate-able.

Like that's what drinking beer will do for you? Wrong.

Enthusiastic indulgence in beer will make you fat and stupid. Everybody knows that. How come the nation doesn't rock with derisive laughter every time those ads come on showing guys with snare-drum tight stomachs and women with the perky breasts and the saucy buns?

That has nothing to do with beer. That is the antithesis of the beer experience.

Still we buy it. Or more specifically, we buy the beer. Two hundred and fifty million two-fours a year in this country. That's getting on $5 billion worth of beer annually. No wonder the folks at Labatt and Molson's and Carling O'Keefe don't blink at spending 75 or 80 million bucks a year in advertising.

Doesn't matter that Blue tastes like Ex tastes like Red Cap tastes like Miller Bud Coors Genessee Pabst Blue Ribbon. Doesn't matter a drop. As the president of the advertising agency Vickers and Benson once said, "With beer, you drink the advertising."

No wonder they go to elaborate and expensive lengths to woo us with the charms of Ice Beer, Lite Beer, Near Beer, BE YER OWN DAWG beer and — wait for it — Bimbo Beer.

Yup. Beer for Babes. The latest thing. Suddenly dawned on the moguls of foam that they were missing out on a good 50 percent of the potential guzzling market. To wit: women. Women don't like beer, by and large. Put it down to taste. Put it down to simple observation. Maybe women noticed that beer makes guys fat and stupid. Whatever. Women don't drink the stuff much.

Beer barons hope to change that.

Makes business sense when you think about it. Canadian men can't drink much more beer than they're putting away now. Pilsner is no great shakes as an industrial lubricant and it would only befuddle Fido if it was added to pet food. Women are the last frontier.

Rumours about a new feminine brew have been rife in the beer biz for a long time. The rumours said the beer would sport a more sophisticated label, or would be extra-lite in calories, or would come in smaller, gal-size bottles. 'Cause women, the cute li'l thaings, cain't put it away like men, yuh know.

The hints are getting broader. A recent newspaper ad for Labatt nattered on about the passing of summer . . . and concluded: "Maybe in the near future there'll be another new Labatt beer or two to try."

Mmm hmmm. Maybe. And my hunch is, the pronunciation emphasis on the new Labatt will be decidedly on the "la."

Hip hops for chic chicks. Suds for sisters. Fem froth. Coming soon to a beer store near you. But remember: beer basically makes you fat and stupid.

And if you fall for those beer commercials, well, you're halfway there already.

Dear Innkeeper

You stay in hotels much? I do. More than I'd like to, actually. Sleeping in strange beds under rented sheets with the meter running, as it were, is an odd way to spend one's time when you think about it. Do it too much and it can lead to the development of certain idiosyncrasies.

Take Vicki Gabereau. She says the first thing she does when she gets into a new hotel room is turn on the TV. That's the second thing I do.

The first thing I do is steal the matches.

It's true. I run all around the hotel room gathering up the matchbooks and stuffing them in my suitcase. I don't even smoke. I don't have a fireplace at home. Or any oil lamps. I light maybe half a dozen candles a year, tops. So why do I steal the matches? I have no idea. I control more matchsticks than E.B. Eddy. I own more sulphur than Satan. I can't solve your marital problems or work out your income tax for you, but if you ever need a light, I'm your man.

I don't just spend my hotel time commandeering matchbooks, though. I spend a fair amount of time thinking about what's good about hotel rooms.

And what's not so good.

What's not so good are: windows that don't open, camouflaged thermostats that only James Bond could find, minuscule bath towels, chambermaids who drumknuckle your door at dawn and carol, "ROOOOOOOOOM check!" and radios that never pick up CBC. Why is it that hotel radios never pick up CBC? Is it a Ted Rogers plot? I can get all the country and western, evangelical, "Sex with Sue" hotline, and late-night phone-in shows a body could never ask for . . . but I can never pick up CBC.

Here's another observation — Conrad Hilton, if you're listening —

lose the complimentary shoe mitt. For one thing, most people are wearing Adidas or Nikes or Sauconys these days. And for another thing, the shoe mitts don't even work very well. Ever tried to shine your shoes with one, Conrad? I thought not. Deep-six the shoe mitt.

And while you're at it, why not transform the hotel rooms that are over the disco or next to the ice machine? Why not turn them into towel-storage rooms or something? Nobody wants to try to sleep while LaToya Jackson is whooping and yodelling — or while the ice machine is going BODODODODODODODODODOOODLUMP every twenty minutes. And no hotel guest will ever ever forgive you for sentencing them to those rooms from hell.

And one more suggestion, O, hoteliers and innkeepers of the world. And this one doesn't come from me. It comes from Joseph Brodsky, a Nobel laureate and Poet Laureate of the U.S. of A. Mr. Brodsky died a few years go, but not before he laid his head on more than a few hotel pillows. He knows the sterility of your average hotel room. And he has a solution.

Joseph Brodsky and a friend, Andrew Carroll, conspired to stock hotel rooms with . . . poetry books.

Yes! Anthologies of Emily Dickinson, Walt Whitman, and Robert Frost. Already hotel chains in Massachusetts, Virginia, and Texas have agreed to lay in free books of poetry right alongside the sappy shopping brochures and the chirpy "How're We Doin'?" evaluation questionnaires. The rationale? As Brodsky put it, "When poetry is available you can make a choice between a drug and a book, a gun and a book — God knows what."

Free poetry in the privacy of your hotel room. Sounds like a good deal to me. And God knows Canada has the raw material. Leonard Cohen, Margaret Atwood, Irving Layton, Earle Birney.

I wouldn't be averse to finding Susan Musgrave nestled next to my Gideon the next time I check into a hotel room.

Tell ya what, you hotel keepers, I'll cut you a deal. Give me a little free poetry in my room and I promise to stop stealing your matches.

Welcome to the World World

Of all the developments of the late twentieth century — and I include Michael Jackson and the sex life of Woody Allen here — of all the late-twentieth-century developments, I think none is more bizarre than the proliferation of theme parks.

Florida is the nurse log of theme parks (they call them Worlds in Florida). Down there you can visit Alligator World, Circus World, Jungle World, Sea World, Clock World, Shell World, and of course, Disney World . . . but that's old hat. Florida has taken a quantum leap in the theme-park business. It is now possible to visit Key West World . . . without actually having to go to Key West, Florida.

You have only to go to Orlando, Florida — that's where Key West World is. Then all you have to do is pull out your wallet and buy the whole family tickets to Key West World, a theme park devoted to the highlights of — you know — the actual Key West, just down the road.

Advantages? Well, Key West World will be a lot safer to visit because you won't have to put up with any actual Key West citizens — writers, poets, troubadours, panhandlers, pickpockets, drug runners, assorted crazies who you might find in the real Key West. That's because everybody in Key West World will be an employee of Key West World — interested only in seeing that you have the best possible time your credit limit will allow.

The concept isn't entirely new, of course. For the past two decades, tourists in Orlando have been able to pay pseudo-visits to Britain, Canada, China, France, Germany, Italy, Japan, Mexico, Morocco, and Norway — all without leaving the confines of Epcot Centre. But those are all pretty exotic locales. Key West World represents the first time we've had a city simulate another city in the same state.

123

You realize what this means, don't you? It's a whole new mind warp on the tourism business. You no longer have to *be* anywhere to actually be anywhere. No reason why folks in Kapuskasing couldn't clear a half-dozen hectares of northwestern Ontario bush, bring in a backhoe, divert a river or two, and declare themselves Niagara Falls World. The Drumheller chamber of commerce could whack up some Quonset huts and surplus army tents on a few acres of pasture land outside of town, hand out a few concession licences, and declare it West Edmonton Mall World. (Huh, just watch those Ghermazian brothers chew on their hat brims.)

Heck, we should be thinking globally here. With full-bore virtual reality, a little wall-to-wall Muzak and free margaritas all around, there's no reason why Saskatoon couldn't host a Pamplona Running of the Bulls World. Why Tuktoyaktuk couldn't be home to a Paris in the Spring World. And what's to stop the citizenry of Musquadoboit from becoming New York World? A place to see cardboard mock-ups of the Empire State Building, the Statue of Liberty, and Bob Dylan's brownstone — all without once getting mugged.

This could turn out to be the biggest thing since Mickey met Minnie. The economic shot in the arm we've all been waiting for. A world-wide theme park in which every town and city pretends to be somewhere more exciting, with lots of parking, great rides, and a clean restaurant on every block. It's an idea whose time has come: Nirvana World.

Say, did you want fries with that?

Switch Those Pipes!

I've always had trouble with the bagpipes. What makes it extra troublesome is my genetic lineage. Near as I can figure, I come from a long line of Scottish Lowland sheep molesters. So my heart should quiver at the skirl o' the pipes.

Well, my heart doesn't. But my stomach does.

Bagpipes. Someone once described a gentleman as someone who knows how to play the bagpipes . . . but doesn't. And before my Meridian answering machine clogs up with collect calls placed by out-raged MacMafiosi from Craigellachie, B.C., to Inverness, Nova Scotia, let me hasten to point out that the gentleman who made that observa-tion was one Senator Allan MacEachen, a native Cape Bretoner, who could be counted on to know gentlemen — or a set of bagpipes — when he saw them.

The bagpipes. A great caterwauling curse that's followed me all my life. When I was a kid, there was old Mr. Ritchie, down at the bottom of our street. Three or four times a year, Mr. Ritchie would retire to his cellar to commune with the spirits. A couple of Celtic saints named Haig and Haig. After several hours, he would stagger into his yard, his chapped, knobby knees protruding from under a moth-eaten kilt. He would be carrying bagpipes, which he would then attempt to simultaneously strangle and blow up.

Mr. Ritchie wasn't a very good bagpiper. Or perhaps he was concert quality. That's the thing about bagpipes.

Later I moved to Thunder Bay for thirteen years. Thirteen mostly won-derful years. Except for the lunch hours, Monday to Friday. That's when the piper came out in a park near my radio station to scatter the pigeons and traumatize small children with his mutilation of "Road to the Isles."

People often ask me why I left Thunder Bay. Was it the winters? Was it the Mulroney filleting of CBC regional programming? The Siren call of that painted old hooker on the Humber, Hogtown?

Nah. It was mostly that godforsaken bagpiper in Patterson Park.

How clever of me, then, to leave all that and move to Fergus, Ontario. Fairrrrrrgus. Whose main street is Saint Andrew, named after the patron saint of you know where. Whose emblem is the Scotch thistle! Fairrrrrrrrrgus. Home of the Highland Games, do ye ken. Where, each August, dozens and dozens and dozens and dozens of pipers pipe their Celtoid brains out.

Not without practice, of course. Contrary to the way they sound, the bagpipes require a lot of practice. Why, sometimes the pipers of Fergus don't even wait for the snow to melt before they get out there in their backyards and on the parade grounds, practising for the August Highland Games.

Bagpipes. When you think of it, we Scots have a lot to answer for. What have we given the world? Plaid. Porridge. Haggis.

And bagpipes.

But on the plus side of the ledger: single-malt Scotch. And Robbie Burns.

Even your tight-fisted Scot would have to allow that that's not a bad bargain.

Speaking of which, that may be Scotland's greatest gift to the world. Sociological safety valve. The last national stereotype at which you can safely snicker without being picketed: the penny-pinching Scot.

Two Scots run into each other at the bus station. "Where are ye bound, Jock?" says one.

"I'm off to Graetna Green for my honeymoon," says the other.

"Aye? And where's the bonnie bride?" asks the first.

"Och," says Jock, "*she's* already been to Graetna Green."

Splendid Sendoffs

I just got back from Florida . . . and I'm not bragging.

It wasn't that great. The weather was blech, the beach was mined with nasty little jellyfish, the shopping was no great shakes (unless you were looking for a deal on sequinned T-shirts), and the traffic was worthy of downtown Toronto after a Blue Jays doubleheader.

Ah, but I wouldn't have missed it for the world. Because one day when I was sitting in the coffee shop, I picked up a copy of the *Boca Raton Bugle*.

And read about the funeral service for a Cadillac convertible.

Yessir! Those Americans, God bless 'em, buried a Cadillac Coupe de Ville last month — presiding minister, assembly of graveside mourners — the whole enchilada.

And just to give the ceremony that extra dash of authenticity, they made sure the owner was in the front seat.

Relax, she was dead. As a matter of fact, the woman who owned the Caddy was the real subject of the funeral. Her dying wish was to be buried in her beloved Cadillac. America, Land of Opportunity, obliged.

Not that the Yanks have a lock on bizarre burials. The Russians, after all, packed the carcass of Vladimir Lenin with rock salt and kept it on public display for seventy years after his death.

Then there's Jeremy Bentham. The English philosopher, who died in 1832, willed his entire estate to London Hospital . . . with one provision. Bentham's will insisted that his preserved remains be permitted to preside over all hospital board meetings. The hospital agreed, and Bentham's skeleton was assembled with wires to hold the bones together. The skull was fitted out with a wax mask of the philosopher's face. The "body" was decked out in Bentham's favourite clothes, plopped in an armchair, and set in a glass-fronted mahogany case.

And for the next ninety-two years, Jeremy Bentham "presided" over meetings of the London Hospital board of directors.

To make sure no one was confused, a placard that read Not Voting was placed in front of him.

I think old Jeremy did very well, considering that cremation was not the popular option it is today. Rendering an unwieldy cadaver down to a shot glass full of ashes greatly increases the choices for creative disposal.

Nowadays folks can direct that their ashes be scattered at sea, sprinkled over a golf course, or dug into the vegetable garden. There was a chap in England who willed his ashes to be placed in his favourite bar stool.

And for avid hunters who bite the bullet, there's an entrepreneur in the States who will tamp your ashes into shotgun shells and deliver them to your hunting buddies, who can then blast them reverentially over your favourite hunting area.

There may be a whole new growth industry here. Death 'N Stuff Inc. Or perhaps Stiffs 'R Us. I know there's already a free-enterprise spin to the morgue in Houston, Texas.

It's a gift shop. Right in the morgue. Folks can buy such grisly gizmos as personalized toe tags, or T-shirts and beach towels that feature chalk body outlines.

Sort of a "coroner store," as it were.

Sound absurd? Well, it's no sillier than most of our bizarre burial practices when you think about it.

Reminds me of the story about a Canadian visiting a cemetery to put flowers on his parents' grave. While there, he can't help noticing an old Chinese man placing a bowl of soup on the grave of one of his dearly departed.

Unable to conceal his derision, the Canadian sneers, "When do you think your friend will be up to eat the soup?"

The Chinese murmurs softly, "About the same time your friends show up to smell the flowers."

Skullful Acting

The hours are lousy. The pay in most cases is below minimum wage. You have to deal daily with sleazeballs, scum suckers, and human pond slime who make your average political convention look like a strawberry social. You get to live with cockroaches and bill collectors and landlords who would cheerfully cut out your heart with a bottle opener if you were a day late with the rent. The question is: why would *anybody* want to be . . . an actor?

That's the question.

And the answer is: because it's the biggest ego trip on the Midway of Life. Acting. Hamming it up. Shrieking and pouting and smouldering and raging and hooting and howling and hissing, harrumphing, and generally emoting all over the linoleum at the drop of a stage cue! Who — save those not possessed of a sufficiency of *cojones* — who *wouldn't* want to be an actor?

Mind you, it's a tough gig. Unless you're an Olivier or a Hepburn, you don't get a lot of respect.

Not even from your fellow actors.

"Acting is the most minor of gifts and not a very high-class way to make a living. After all, Shirley Temple could do it at age four."

Did Preston Manning say that? Or Rush Limbaugh? Or Margaret Thatcher? Nope. Katharine Hepburn said that.

Acting. It's a bit like professional baseball. You're either a great — or a grunt. Which brings us to the case of Jonathan Hartman, thirty-nine-year-old Canadian actor, presently subsisting in London, who is tired of spear-chucking, hatchet-handling, also-ranning, and otherwise second banana-ing in theatrical productions. Mr. Hartman has taken the thespian bull by the terpsichorean horns. He has bequeathed his plucked head to the Royal Shakespeare Company to appear as the skull of Yorick in all future productions of *Hamlet*.

You know Yorick? Hamlet fondles his skull briefly in act 5, scene 1, and says soliloquy-ishly, "Alas! Poor Yorick. I knew him, Horatio."

Doesn't matter. Point is, young Johnny Hartman figured a sure-fire shortcut to theatrical immortality would be to have his noggin appear in every production of *Hamlet,* henceforth and hereafter.

He's put it in his will — a codicil of which states: "Because of my love of classical theatre . . . I have decided, given the transitory nature of employment so common to my profession, to ensure myself a perpetual, albeit posthumous engagement . . ."

And a good idea it was. Except that the Royal Shakespeare Company has declined Jonathan Hartman's request. They prefer poor Yorick's noodle to be made of plastic. "We couldn't use a real skull on stage," they explain, "as bone is too brittle and the skull gets some rough handling."

Alas, poor Hartman. He's not the first unknown to take a run at the gates of Ham Heaven. There is the story of a young Peter O'Toole, who landed a bit part as a Georgian peasant in a play by Chekov. All the fledgling O'Toole had to say was "Doctor Ostroff! The horses are ready!" But the young O'Toole was no fool. He knew this was his chance at greatness. He contrived to make his young, anonymous peasant look like Stalin, the sweep-broom moustache, the shock of black hair — he even worked up a slight limp like Stalin's. He rehearsed Stalin's vocal inflections, his demeanour, his hatred and furious resentment of his tsarist overlords. All this O'Toole planned to pack into his six-word speech "Dr. Ostro . . ." The first-nighters in London were duly impressed by this scowling, fulminating, ominous, suddenly portentous figure who burst upon the stage. O'Toole, transformed into a swarthy Georgian warlord, faced the audience, inhaled, and — speaking in clear, ringing tones from the diaphragm — intoned: "Doctor Horsey! The Ostroffs are ready!"

Jerry's Dead — Again

Life certainly has some kinky ways of reminding a body that the clock is ticking. Could be the voluptuous fan who leans close and whispers huskily, "My parents love listening to your show." Could be that little *son et lumière* display that detonates behind your eyeballs when you bend over to tie up a shoelace.

Or it could be picking up the morning paper and reading that Jerry Rubin's dead.

Yes, that Jerry Rubin. He of the Chicago Seven. Of Dollar Day Madness at the New York Stock Exchange. Of Yippies and campus cut-ups and running pigs for president.

Dead at fifty-six. Hit by a car while crossing a street in L.A.

Of course, the famous counterculture Jerry Rubin had already been dead for some time. The Jerry Rubin who got clipped by a car crossing Wiltshire Boulevard was not wearing a beard or a Windy Puff hairdo or love beads or a bullet bandoleer or a cape made from a North Vietnamese flag. No, the Jerry Rubin that left us behind was suited up in a three-piece, short hair, tie snugged up flush to the Adam's apple, chunky cuff links, shiny Gucci's. Looked for all the world like a Wall Street venture capitalist — which, in fact, he was.

What a strange and untrackable roller-coaster ride this guy took. What social commentator in their wildest acid hallucination would have dreamt that the Che Guevara lookalike screaming in a Chicago courtroom in 1969 would be cultivating an ulcer while squinting at stock quotations in the canyons of Wall Street twenty years later?

Maybe it's fitting that Rubin Two ended up in the coiled embrace of something as ethereal, as intangible, as the stock market — chasing non-existent sow bellies and chimerical pork futures — because Jerry

Rubin One never did very much you could actually lay your hands on either.

About all we have left of the early model is . . . air. Slogans, pronouncements, some of them breathtakingly idiotic. Rubin the revolutionary is the guy who said, "I fell in love with his cherub face and sparkling eyes . . . his words and courage inspire us."

He was talking about Charlie Manson.

He made a few other axiomatic contributions.

Who was it that said, "I'm famous . . . that's my job"?

Jerry Rubin One.

Who said, "Don't trust anyone over thirty"?

Jerry Rubin One.

Who amended that two decades later to "Don't trust anyone *under* fifty"?

Jerry Rubin Two.

Who said, "Look both ways before you cross the street"?

Elmer the Safety Elephant.

Jerry, you weren't listening.

You Cane Do That in Singapore

Punishment is a sort of medicine.

ARISTOTLE

Thinking of visiting Singapore someday? Maybe taking the kids along? Here are a couple of no-no's you may want to bring to their attention before you take off for a day's sightseeing.

Do not drop litter.

Do not feed the pigeons.

Do not spit on the sidewalk.

Do not eat while driving.

Do not pick the flowers.

Do not chew gum.

And lest your kids think these are just wishful guidelines like the Don't Walk signs at Canadian stoplights, you might want to tell them that the fine for, say, chewing gum or feeding pigeons in Singapore is a flat thousand dollars. No court-appointed lawyer. No case workers or appeals. Just a thousand bucks — pay up or go to jail.

And you *really* don't want to go to jail in Singapore.

Well, what do you expect? Singapore is not an advanced, sophisticated nation like Canada. It's a tight-sphinctered police state of 2 million souls crammed onto an island not much bigger than some Saskatchewan wheat farms and surrounded by potentially hostile neighbours.

That makes for a nervous government. Nervous about a lot of things. Drugs, for instance. A few years ago, heroin started to show up in Singapore. The government came up with a very simple solution: billboards. Billboards all over Singapore. You can see them when you get off the plane. The billboards say simply: Warning: Death for Drug Dealers Under Singapore Law.

They mean it, too. Get caught dealing dope in Singapore and all the Melvin Bellis and Eddie Greenspans in the world will not come between you and your date with the Singapore hangman.

And don't expect special attention just because you carry a passport identifying you as a privileged citizen of a progressive Western country. Michael Fay found that out the hard way. Fay is the American kid who went on a rampage in downtown Singapore, spray-painting parked cars and slinging eggs and bricks around. The Singapore courts sentenced him to five lashes.

Which, in Singapore, is more than enough. They use a rattan cane on the bare buttocks, wielded by a martial-arts expert. Lashees usually lose consciousness after the first couple of strokes.

Predictably, many Americans objected to the harsh penalty. Boys will be boys, they said. Even President Clinton suggested that the punishment was out of proportion to the crime.

Singapore went ahead and lashed.

Barbaric? Some folks think so. On the other hand, political corruption is virtually unheard of in Singapore. The streets are spotless and utterly safe to walk at any hour (unless Michael Fay's about). There are no slums, and the people of Singapore enjoy a health-care system that would bring tears to the eyes of Tommy Douglas. Singapore must be one of the few countries in the world that has no — repeat, *no* — hard drug problem. Other crimes? Vandalism, robbery, and rape are all "caneable" offences. There hasn't been a bank robbery in years. Singapore hasn't had to increase the size of its police force since 1967.

Meanwhile, Michael Fay hails from a country where John Wayne Gacy, who murdered thirty-three kids, was put to death by injection thirteen *years* after he was found guilty.

Thirteen years. That's more time than some of his victims had on the planet.

And here in Canada, taxpayers still pick up the tab for a piece of human flotsam named Clifford Olsen, a serial child-killer who sits in a prison cell with a TV and a computer and a telephone on which he chats with anyone who'll accept his calls.

So whose system is better — Singapore's or ours? Well, it's hard to deal in absolutes, but let me leave you with one.

I am absolutely sure that if Michael Fay ever goes on a vandalizing binge again, it won't be in Singapore.

Break This Chain

It could happen to you the next time you pick up your mail.

There, nestled in among the grocery-store flyers and the dreaded envelopes with ominous cellophane windows, you spy a letter with a strange postmark and an unfamiliar return address. Curious, you tear it open.

And find yourself reading a chain letter.

But this one's a different kind of chain letter. It doesn't promise you untold riches or a fabulous sex life or an eternity of foul luck if you don't send off copies to six other unsuspecting saps.

No, this chain letter tells you the heartbreaking story of little Craig Shergold. Craig is a seven-year-old British schoolboy, says the letter. It also tells you that Craig has an inoperable brain tumour and only one wish in the world.

Craig wants to be in *The Guinness Book of Records*. He hopes to get there by becoming the human being to receive the most mail in history.

And you can help, the letter says. Just drop him a line — or just address an envelope and pop your business card inside.

Jeez, it's little enough to ask for a kid who's dying, right?

Well, I've got five words of advice for you should you receive this letter.

Throw it in the garbage.

Sound heartless? Hey, if Craig Shergold could talk to you, he would *beg* you to throw it in the garbage. Yes, there really is a Craig Shergold, and he really did have a dream of getting into *The Guinness Book of Records*. But that was away back in 1989. Before the dream turned into a kind of nightmare.

Craig's letter touched a lot of hearts. Within weeks of his sending his request to a few local newspapers, the lad's local post office in Carshalton, England, was inundated with letters addressed to Craig Shergold.

Before long, the post office was receiving 600 sacks of mail.

Every *day*.

Part of the problem was that Craig wasn't just a U.K. phenomenon. His letter came to the attention of a group called the Children's Wish Foundation in Atlanta, Georgia, which tries to grant the wishes of terminally ill children. It decided to alert the business executives of the continent to Craig's project.

That was several years and tens of millions of cards and letters ago.

"We've got a 10,000-square-foot warehouse that is stacked to the ceiling with mail that still hasn't been opened," moans Arthur Stein, president of the foundation. "There's no way to stop it. Everyone keeps saying quit, and people ignore the pleas."

It's become so bad in Britain that the post office has assigned Craig Shergold his own personal postal code — an honour usually reserved for large towns or counties.

So has the Craig Shergold letter just been a giant migraine for all concerned? On the contrary. This is one chain letter that actually delivered — albeit in ways no one ever intended.

For one thing, Craig Shergold did make *The Guinness Book of Records*. It happened in 1991 when his mail topped the 30 million mark. (Guinness authorities shrewdly retired the category so they wouldn't have to go through this again.)

For another thing, it looks like Craig's condition is cured. An American billionaire, John W. Kluge, read of the boy's plight and paid for him to be flown over and treated by a neurosurgeon in Virginia. More than 90 percent of Craig's brain tumour was removed, and the doctors pronounced him cured.

But the mail just keeps on flooding in.

So if you get a copy of the Craig Shergold chain letter, do the world a favour. Chuck it in the recycling box.

Craig Shergold would thank you for it if he could.

And so would the besieged employees of the Children's Wish Foundation.

Not to mention the forests of the world.

136

What's "Flog" Spelled Backwards?

The Scots have had a lot of good chuckles at the expense of the rest of the human race — bagpipes, haggis, anything plaid, to name just three — but surely their ultimate snicker has to be the game of golf.

Golf. "A game," as Winston Churchill observed, "the aim of which is to hit a very small ball into an even smaller hole with weapons singularly ill-designed for the purpose."

I do not, in case you missed the bias, play golf myself. I consider it a character deficit on a par (if you will) with not playing the accordion or not breeding newts. But I'm not a fanatic about it. Some of my best friends, et cetera. Thus it was that I found myself last weekend standing in the clubhouse of my local golf course with a friend who has the disease. He wanted to know what it would cost to join the club. He asked the golf pro. The initiation fee is $1,900, the golf pro said.

Nineteen hundred bucks! And that only gives you the right to fork out twenty-five or thirty more bucks every time you decide to play!

Nineteen hundred bucks! And we were not standing in the cathedral surroundings of Glen Abbey or Pebble Beach here. This was a modest little local golf course that has never felt the spikes of a Nicholas or a Palmer or a Norman puncturing its turf.

I murmured to my friend that perhaps the golf pro had been nibbling mushrooms at the nineteenth hole. He looked at me as if I'd just crawled out from under a cabbage leaf after a forty-year snooze. "Nineteen hundred's not bad," my friend said. "You know what you pay to play in Japan?"

Well, I didn't. But I've done some checking . . . and nineteen hundred bucks is beginning to look like a golf give-away. There are 12 million golf maniacs in Japan — and not nearly enough open land to keep them all on golf courses. Accordingly, the price for a club membership can go as high as — I swear I'm not making this up — $250,000 (U.S.) — *per year.*

The price of a round of golf in Japan is so stratospheric that Japanese golfers often book a flight to Thailand or Malaysia, play a couple of rounds, and then fly home again. It's cheaper.

I'm afraid I will never comprehend golfing dedication of that magnitude. But then, of course, I couldn't understand about Rabbi Fineberg either. I mean, there he was, a member of an extremely conservative Jewish synagogue . . . out on the local golf course on a Saturday, the Jewish Sabbath — teeing off. Granted, it was at the break of dawn. The rabbi probably figured there'd be no one around to see him, but he was wrong. Bishop O'Malley was there, creeping through the underbrush, bird-watching, as is the bishop's wont.

Well, as the bishop told me later, he was paralyzed with shock at the sight of the rabbi standing at the first tee. He dropped to his knees on the spot and moaned, "Oh, God, he's a very religious man. Why are you permitting this?"

To the bishop's astonishment a voice rang out: "He will be dealt with appropriately!"

As the bishop watched, the rabbi teed off, smacked a beautiful, soaring, straight-as-a-die shot that arced up like a rainbow over the water hazard, past the sand trap, plopped to the green, bounced once, twice, and then right into the hole.

The bishop cried out, "Lord, is this how you punish him? The rabbi makes a spectacular hole-in-one on his first shot?"

And the voice answers: "And who is he going to tell?"

Bruno's Revenge

I don't know about you, but I have a problem with hunting. I know it's hypocritical. I like moose sausage and I've chewed my way through my share of wild duck, jugged hare, and venison steak.

I also know what goes on in abattoirs and "meat processing" plants. And some of my best friends own shotguns and rifles with telescopic sights, and they go out in the bush and put them to their intended use every hunting season.

I don't begrudge them that. I just can't do it myself is all. Aside from one rabid fox and an old cat with distemper, I don't think I've ever personally met a critter I thought had less of a right to live than I do.

Then there's the deer herd that hangs out in an orchard across the street from my house. They are about as "wild" as my aunt Beulah's parakeet. Whenever I leave my front gate open, they wander in and browse on my rose bushes with all the nonchalance of paying tenants. They're pesky and annoying, but I can't imagine unlimbering a thirty-ought-six and blowing them away.

So I'm too wimpy to hunt. But I keep abreast of the hunting news. And I am curiously gratified to be able to report two new hunting initiatives that have made the headlines — and my day — recently.

One concerns fox hunting, a sport that Oscar Wilde defined as the unspeakable in pursuit of the uneatable. And indeed the pursuit of a twenty-pound fox with hounds and horses until it drops from exhaustion is a pastime one would have to be seriously warped to support. Until now. The latest development in fox hunting doesn't feature a fox at all. It features joggers. Human marathon runners are given a sporting head start. They galumph on foot across meadows and fields with the hounds and hunters in hot pursuit. Best part of the revised fox hunt is that the quarry doesn't get ripped to pieces at the end. Each runner carries a doggie bag of treats. The hounds that track them down get dog biscuits as a reward.

The other hunting development occurred closer to home. The British Columbia Ministry of the Environment has announced that black and grizzly bears seemed to have made a startling new environmental adaptation. They are learning to associate the sound of gunshots with a free meal. Lately, more and more hunters have been rudely interrupted while dressing out deer, elk, and moose carcasses by black bears and grizzlies showing up ready to chow down.

And the bears aren't really particular as to whether they feast on elk haunch or brisket of hunter.

Gruesome? Yeah, I suppose so. But I can't help feeling a frisson of satisfaction that some nimrods are at last finding out what it feels like to be on the losing end of the usually loaded hunting equation.

Reminds me of the story intoned by an evah-so-propah British news announcer on a BBC Television newscast.

"A man out hunting in the Highlands today climbed over a fence with his rifle cocked.

"He is survived by his wife, three children, and one pheasant."

PART 5

Ah, I Remember It Well . . .

Door to Door Is Dead

You know what you're never going to discover any more when you answer a knock at your front door? A door-to-door encyclopedia salesman. They are extinct. Vaporized. The American headquarters of Encyclopedia Britannica just officially laid off all of its home-sales representatives.

Which is not exactly a 9.9 on the Richter calamity scale for most of us — unless you happen to be a door-to-door encyclopedia salesman.

I was, once. For one night. Answered an ad in the *Globe and Mail* that promised high wages, free training, and great hours, no experience necessary. Just the kind of job I was looking for — and was qualified to do. Especially the "no experience" part.

It turned out to be the Encyclopedia Britannica folks — or rather, the rottweilerish sales agency EB depended on to get their product to the public. These guys accepted as salesmen all warm bodies without visible drug habits who didn't look like axe murderers, and they put us through an intensive one-day training course that drilled into our skulls the infrangible, two-pronged secret of selling encyclopedias door to door: never stop smiling and never stop talking.

Also . . . never deviate from the script, which we had to memorize. It was about three pages long and, the drill sergeant in charge of our indoctrination seminar assured us, written by a fully qualified psychiatrist.

What that script was, was dumb. Illogical, cliché-raddled, and mind-paralyzingly monotonous — but curiously effective. A salesman could be pretty sure that if he got to the end of page three without having to eat a door knocker or duck an airborne ashtray, he had a sale.

However, a salesman didn't often get to the end of page three. You didn't often get to the end of "Good evening, sir . . . I'm taking a survey on readership habits and I wondered if — (SLAM).

A very dispiriting experience, my one-day career as a door-to-door encyclopedia salesman. I hadn't been rebuffed that many times since the spot dance at the senior prom. Door-rapping drummers were not a popular species even way back then. Things must be even worse now if Encyclopedia Britannica, the king of foot-in-the-door marketing, is finally throwing in the towel.

The thing I could never figure out was: why did Encyclopedia Britannica sell its books door to door in the first place? The company had a great product. Why didn't it just set up displays in Coles and Chapters and Eaton's and the Bay, and sell it the normal way? Why did EB need polyester-clad hounds from hell like me flogging volumes through the front-door mail slot?

Well, turns out it didn't. Encyclopedia Britannica is now going the conventional route — shopping malls, home-shopping networks, and catalogues. They won't miss me as a rep.

I was absolutely useless at it — that's why my sales career aborted in twenty-four hours — but I confess to a grudging admiration for the ones who could do it. Guys schlepping up driveway after driveway with a sample box and a Think Positive attitude. Often possessing no marketable skills other than a refusal to say uncle, pumped up by some self-hypnotic, crazy, kamikaze, upbeat sort of optimism . . . sailing along, as Willy Loman, the patron schlump of door-to-door salesmen put it, in *Death of a Salesman,* "on a smile and a shoeshine."

Times change, I guess. Today if you said "smile and a shoeshine," some Generation Xer might respond, "Shoeshine . . . shoeshine? How do you shine a Nike?"

Radio Daze

I'm a lucky guy because I work in the media. Don't let anybody kid you — it's a wonderful way to turn a buck.

Sure, I'll never be rich, but on the other hand there's no dress code. I get to shoot my mouth off. And I meet a helluva lot of interesting folks.

I also get to explore the fascinating differences among the "media." I write a newspaper column, I host a weekly radio show, and every once in a while I do a spot of television.

And just as in all families, each brother and sister is as different as different can be.

Writing a newspaper column is very satisfying. I get to put words together on whatever bee is currently rattling around in my bonnet as best I can and splay them out on half a page of sixty-odd newspapers every week.

Molson or Esso would pay big bucks for that space. I get it for free.

Television? That's another story. It is at once the most powerful and least satisfying of all the media I know. People watch you on television but they don't necessarily listen to what you have to say. I remember the first time I went on the tube. The producers told me I had exactly ninety seconds to make whatever point it was I was trying to make. I slaved over my words like a poet seducing a lover. I wrote. I got made up. I read my words off the AutoCue. The next day I asked my friends what they thought.

They all replied, "Where'd you get that ugly sports jacket?"

That's the thing about television. It is enormously, overpoweringly visual. You could go on TV and recite the first four pages of the Hamilton telephone book and nobody would notice — as long as you looked like Brad Pitt or Pamela Anderson.

And radio? Ah, radio. I beg the editor's indulgence — what I am about to type is not what a print person wants to read — but radio is the most satisfying medium to write for.

Because in radio you get to use people's heads. There is no need to spend thousands of dollars constructing a film set of the Nile delta or downtown Winnipeg. All you have to do in radio is say, "Yellowknife . . . January . . . 1945" — and the listeners' brains fill in the details!

Radio is magic. Radio is make-believe.

Radio is, of course, not what it once was.

People like to think that radio, like everything else, has got better, subtler, more sophisticated as time passes.

But actually, radio has got worse.

The fact is, back in the old days you could pull in marvellous things on your radio set. As Torontonian Ron Haggart, another old-timer, wrote in the *Globe and Mail* recently, "As a child in Vancouver . . . I could easily listen to KSL, Salt Lake City . . . even WBZ, a continent away in Boston was possible . . . and of course the Canadian Broadcasting Corporation's famous clear-channel station at Watrous, Saskatchewan. . . ."

Ah, yes. The good old days. For old-time, dyed-in-the-vacuum-tube radio fans, I heartily recommend a book by Garrison Keillor called *WLT.* It is a paean to the salad days of radio, and it contains this passage:

> *Oh, the days when radio was new. . . . It was so beautiful. Back then, the radio signal was received all the way to the Alleghenies and west to the Rockies. . . . Radio spanned the continent, and radios were built to pull in signals from far away. The Zenith had a tuning knob as big as a grapefruit. You'd spin that and bring in Nashville and Cincinnati and Detroit and Little Rock and Salt Lake City and Pittsburgh. These little dinky pisspot radios you buy today won't get a signal from 30 miles away, and why should they? The shows sound the same everywhere you go. . . . Radio used to be a dream and now it's a jukebox. . . . But of course if you climb on your high horse and talk about radio when it amounted to something, people mark you down as an old fart, the sort who grumbles about the decline of railroad travel and circuses. . . .*

Amen. If you disagree, send a letter, care of the publisher.

Care to Dance?

There's a little snatch of William Butler Yeats rattling around in my head today. It's from a poem of his called "Among Schoolchildren." The only lines I can remember go:

O chestnut-tree, great-rooted blossomer,
Are you the leaf, the blossom or the bole?
O body swayed to music, O brightening glance,
How can we know the dancer from the dance?

The dancer from the dance. Strikes me that in the half-century or so since Yeats penned those lines, it has become even harder to tell the dancer from the dance.

More and more we seem to want to blur the lines between imitation and reality. Think of Disney World, with its imitation frontier and its imitation jungle and its imitation — everything.

Think of the West Edmonton Mall, with its imitation beach and its imitation ocean and even imitation waves. Think of Skydome, pretending to be a baseball park. Think of . . . well, think of the Christmas party I went to last winter. Big family do, lots of folks, including at least a half-dozen healthy teenage boys in attendance. An ice rink in the backyard with homemade goal nets and a bouquet of ready-for-use hockey sticks sticking out of a snowbank . . . and not a single kid to be seen. I found them eventually. They were all upstairs in a bedroom, hunkered down around a computer monitor. The kids were waiting their turn to play a Sega electronic hockey game. Hey, I watched for a few minutes. Incredible. The players on the screen carried the names of actual players in the NHL. The game featured whistles, face-offs, slapshots, cheers, body checks . . . even grunts from body-check victims. The kids were hypnotized. I was entranced. We were watching a game of electronic hockey. We could have been playing the real thing outside. Dancer? Or dance?

Reminded me of something I saw this past summer, out with the dog for an early morning walk on a beautiful day, warm, sunny, birds clearing their gizzards to sing, chattering squirrels bad-mouthing my dog. Still too early for the annoying sounds of car tires or car horns or heat bugs.

Almost silent, except for that persistent whirr coming from that screened-in front porch over there. Squinting, I can just make out a guy in sweats hunched over . . . an exercise bike. Here is a fitness buff, on a beautiful summer morning, sweating and cycling to nowhere on his front porch. Why not live a little? Ride a real bike down the road?

Pretty soon we won't have to even throw our leg over an Exercycle or pick up a Sega joystick or book a ticket for Disney World. All we'll have to do is put on a pair of virtual reality glasses and dial up the daydream of our choice.

Well, sure. Watching that Sega hockey game convinced me that it's only a matter of time before they come out with VR glasses so good you really won't be able to tell imitation from reality. Someday everybody in the whole damn world will be truly out of it, in their perfect VR glasses.

Except you and me, of course. The rest of humanity will be lying around like so many nearsighted zombies, and you and I, we'll still be taking early morning walks.

Maybe we'll meet out there one morning. Listening to real birds and squirrels, watching the real sun rise.

You know what I'll say if I meet you out there one morning?

I'll say: "May I have this dance?"

Who's for the Beach?

I've been feeling more and more excited this morning and I didn't until just a few moments ago figure out why. You know what it is? Summer vacation. Sure. It's the end of June, when for all my school years, the books got shelved and the good clothes moved to the back of the closet and a summer of fishing and biking and generally hanging out beckoned alluringly.

It was also on a weekend morning just like this that Old Man Howarth was apt to look up from his easy chair in front of the TV and say, "Who wants to go to the beach?"

Old Man Howarth — we'd never call him that to his face, he'd have cuffed us — was my boyhood pal Doug Howarth's dad. He was a tall man with a hawk nose and wavy black hair and a boat prow of a moustache that looked like it was swiped from a janitor's broom. He drank O'Keefe Ale and smoked Export Plain. Drank more beer and smoked more cigarettes than any mortal I've seen before or since. But I never saw him drunk or heard him cough.

I think Old Man Howarth and his wife, Clara, were the most naturally gregarious people I ever met. You could literally walk up to their door, go in, take your shoes off, and sit in the living room watching TV . . . or just yak. The Howarths would always be glad to see you. You could make yourself a sandwich, help yourself to a beer (or a pop, depending on your age), and stay as long as you liked. You didn't have to perform or answer any questions . . . and if you stayed past their bedtime, that was no problem. The Howarths would say goodnight and go to bed, trusting you'd turn off the TV and turn out the lights when you left. If you left.

You wouldn't believe the people that passed through Old Man

Howarth's front room. Kids and adults. Dogs, cats. Shy young things and high-school sophomores in heat. Policemen, sales reps, housewives, farm boys, soldiers, sailors, the slow kid from down the street.

Everybody came to the Howarths because, unlike home or school or work, it was such a nice, comfortable, undemanding place to be.

And the Howarths were always there. Except, as I say, when every once in a while Old Man Howarth would lower a still-foaming O'Keefe empty to the linoleum beside his chair and say, "Who wants to go to the beach?"

And whoever was in the living room and didn't have anywhere they had to be for a couple or three days would pile into Old Man Howarth's station wagon — a beige Chevy Biscayne — with bathing suits, blankets, maybe a baseball and a couple of mitts, a crib board for the oldsters, a hamper full of food — and off everyone would go to Wasaga Beach. It was only about seventy miles, but sometimes it'd take us two days to get there. We travelled like gypsies. Picnics in churchyards. Afternoon naps under shady trees. Overnights in gravel pits and alongside abandoned barns, all of us crammed like cordwood into the back of the station wagon, trying to get to sleep before Old Man Howarth started to snore.

Funny . . . I remember the trips to the beach better than the beach itself. The brown ribbon of backroad, the dust balloons billowing out behind us, the keening of heat bugs and the whiny protest of the engine as the Chevy laboured along, mile after mile, in second gear.

Never in a hurry was Old Man Howarth.

Funny. Every once in a while, often in February, my friends and I fall to musing and play a game called Where Would You Like to Be Right Now? Some people choose a beach in Crete, others say a château in Whistler or a cabin in Temagami or a restaurant off the Via Veneto.

But I can never seem to do much better than the lumpy green couch in Old Man Howarth's living room.

Unless maybe it's the back seat of a Chevy Biscayne crawling along a backroad towards Wasaga Beach.

A Prairie Treasure

Last Saturday evening I was at a dinner in the Wildrose Ballroom out in Edmonton, Alberta, sitting across the table from the hands-down funniest, and quite possibly the wisest, writer Canada ever spawned. I was sitting there looking across at W.O. Mitchell, and I was thinking about "The Love Song of J. Alfred Prufrock."

You know, the poem with the line that goes: *"I grow old . . . I grow old . . . I shall wear the bottoms of my trousers rolled."*

T.S. Eliot wrote the lines about eighty-five years ago. A retired Pierre Elliott Trudeau quoted the lines a few years back when he surfaced in Ottawa to maul the Tory carcass one last time.

And last Saturday night, at the Alberta Book Awards banquet in Edmonton, W.O. Mitchell . . . W.O. Mitchell *looked* the lines.

Well, I couldn't see if the bottoms of his trousers were rolled, but he looked a little shrivelled in his suit, the way elder statesmen sometimes do. Listing a little to port — and towards the quite wonderful and ageless Merna, whom W.O. has referred to as his "biological relation by marriage" for more than fifty years.

W.O. was wearing a plaster cast on his left hand and a hearing aid in his right ear. His Leacockian thatch of silver hair looked like it had seen perhaps a little too much wind.

And . . . he was wearing a pink bib. A big shave-and-a-haircut style bib tucked into the neck of his shirt and fanned right across his torso.

Ah, well. The frailties of age, eh?

Shall I part my hair behind? Do I dare to eat a peach? W.O. passed on the romaine lettuce tossed in tarragon vinaigrette with tomatoes in favour of a little silver coke spoon, which he produced from his breast pocket, filled with snuff, and hoovered up his nostrils from time to time. His eyes were bright and he responded when spoken to, but he did not partake much in the table banter. I think perhaps he couldn't hear all that well.

Well, hell, the man was eighty years old. He's stooked hay, chased cattle, gone to sea, taught school, and even lived in Toronto for a spell, when he wasn't writing novels, plays, and short stories.

Man's entitled to slip a notch or two after a life like that.

Not that it's over. Mr. Mitchell may have been navigating through his anecdotage, but the awards kept cascading in. Order of Canada. Two Leacock medals. An NFB documentary. And he was guest of honour at this Alberta literary banquet in order to receive the Golden Pen Award — a kind of lifetime recognition of what the man has meant to Canada in general and to Albertans most of all.

After Alberta's other poets and novelists and editors and publishers have been acknowledged and awarded, there is a hush and the special moment of the evening is here. W.O. Mitchell's many accomplishments and honours are chronicled. He is given a standing ovation and — oh, dear, he's coming up to the stage . . . let's hope it's not too . . . embarrassing.

Hah! W.O. strides up to the stage, bib billowing, eyes twinkling. He plants a lusty buss on the lips of the woman presenting the award, turns and grips the lectern like a ship's wheel, and says in that squeaky garden-gate voice he puts on: "You know, Merna got me to wear this bib because she got tired of seeing me come home from book tours with snuff stains all down my front. And I told her, 'Merna, it's the darndest thing. . . . I notice that whenever I spill snuff on my front, these lovely young women who are talking to me will just kind of unconsciously brush it off with their hands!'

"And as the book tours wore on, I found I was just kind of unconsciously dropping the snuff lower and lower."

Ah. W.O. Mitchell. It would be a foolhardy do-gooder who would try to roll the bottoms of his trousers for him just yet.

Remembering "the Yards"

You may have missed it in the general din of year-end celebrations on New Year's Eve, but there was a particular burst of good cheer not far from deepest downtown Toronto . . . right about the corner of Keele and St. Clair, to be precise. There was a couple of dozen, maybe thirty, celebrants, but they weren't toasting the New Year or singing "Auld Lang Syne." They weren't nibbling on cocktail wieners or pâté and crackers either. These party people were vegans. Not meat eaters. And they were rejoicing over the death of the Ontario Public Stockyards.

That's right. As of January 1, Toronto has about thirty-five acres of prime land to toy with. Well-fertilized land too. Cattle have been shipped and penned and bought and sold on that thirty-five acres since 1903.

It's hard to wax really romantic about stockyards — which, when all is said and done, are basically holding tanks for slaughterhouses — but the Ontario Public Stockyards wasn't quite the agricultural Auschwitz that the vegans like to paint it. And for a change, I actually know what I'm talking about, because I worked at the Ontario Public Stockyards.

No choice. You heard of Black Brothers Livestock, Inc.? Well, that was my old man. And his brothers — Jack, who was tougher than steak from a seed bull; Jim, who looked like he'd rather be collecting stamps; and good old Uncle Dryden, who was somewhat erratic, perpetually red-faced, and, inevitably, nicknamed Pinky. Pinky Black.

Anyway, the Ontario Public Stockyards is where, as a teenager, I earned my pocket money and picked up a good deal of what passes for my education. I learned, for instance, that although cows don't often kick you, when they do, it comes a lot faster and hurts a helluva lot more than a horse kick. It's that cloven-hoof action cattle have.

153

I learned that, stereotypes notwithstanding, bulls, steers, cows, and calves were well-treated at the stockyards. Lots of hay, plenty of water . . . no rough stuff — after all, who's going to buy damaged goods? Oh, they'd get hee'd and haw'd and prodded with the indispensable cattle cane when they started galloping off in the wrong direction . . . with cattle you're not dealing with Rin Tin Tin, you know. Very little Rhodes Scholarship material between those horns. They're big and they're not bright and they can be frustrating. Still, of the tens of thousands of head of cattle I saw go by, I saw only one treated badly. When a broad-shouldered cockney lout by the name of Davey smacked a steer viciously over the snout with his cane. Bad luck for the steer — worse for Davey because my father saw it too, and fired him on the spot.

There was no killing done in the Ontario Public Stockyards. That was done across the street at Swifts and Canada Packers. Twice a day you could watch the street cars and trucks halt on St. Clair Avenue to let a caravan of cattle make that one-way trip from stockyards to abattoir. Watching that procession of beef on the hoof docilely plodding behind what we called the Judas Steer — the only beast that did get to make the return trip — taught me some kind of a lesson in moral relativity that I'm still mulling over.

But that was a quarter of a century ago. You'd never see animals walking into a slaughterhouse these days. We're more sensitive. We prefer not to meet our meat until it's vacuum packed in airtight plastic and laid out on neat Styrofoam trays or safely tucked away out of sight under a sprig of lettuce in a sesame-seed bun. Yeah, the old Ontario Public Stockyards, just sitting out there at Keele and St. Clair, was an anachronism, for sure. Not many people will miss it, I guess . . . but I will. And curiously enough, one of the things I'll miss most is the smell of the place. Not the stink. That was Canada Packers. The stockyards emanated a heady blend of pipe tobacco, baled hay, male sweat, cheap cigars, and nine decades of cattle manure. I miss it already.

I'll never be able to explain that to a city person.

And to anybody who knew the Ontario Public Stockyards, I won't have to.

Let Your Fingers Do the Walking

The archbishop of Canterbury once huffily declared, "I never read advertisements. I would spend all my time wanting things."

Easy to see the archbishop of Canterbury never lived on Saltspring Island. That's where I live now. Am living now. Am learning to live now. On a wee island in the Georgia Strait nestled between Vancouver the island and Vancouver the city. And though I am a wet-behind-the-ears, green-as-grass neophyte Saltspringer, I have no hesitation in recommending for the archbishop a lifetime subscription to the Saltspring Island telephone directory.

The Saltspring Island telephone directory isn't what you'd call heavy reading — about the size of the book of Leviticus, maybe. But I think it might well change his grace's mind about advertising forever.

See, what I'm beginning to realize about Saltspringers is that they don't take themselves terribly seriously. Thus if you find yourself with bicycle woes on the island, you hie yourself off to the Spoke Folk. If your gas eater is suffering from tire troubles, you would give the Tread Shed a call.

Need your chimney reamed? Then call Hogan Chimney Sweeps. Hogan promises "a cure for the flue." Looking for a hammock? The firm you want is Out on a Limb, Inc. You detect a certain existential angst percolating through the Saltspring telephone directory. This is where Jean-Paul Sartre or William S. Burroughs would have let their fingers do the walking. Dithering over a choice of contractors that range from Hopeless Construction Limited to Bent Nail Home Renovations. Pondering whether a company that calls itself Beancounter Graphics could handle their literary layout problems.

I can especially see William S. Burroughs blending in seamlessly on

Saltspring. First thing he'd probably do after a Naked Lunch would be to get his patio overhauled by Wilderness Stone Works — motto: Why Settle for Less? Get Stoned With the Best.

Then there's Ritchie Bragg, your island auto mechanic. Ritchie doesn't bother with business cards as such, but he does have a promotional T-shirt. It shows a cartoon of a mechanic (presumably Ritchie) flat on his back on one of those dollies mechanics use. He is working with a sprocket wrench on the . . . nether regions of a large cartoon Saltspring Island sheep and he's muttering, "Ah, I see the problem — these nuts have fallen off."

A Saltspring Historical Society? No. But there is a listing for the Saltspring *Hysterical* Society. It's a comedy troupe. A very funny comedy troupe. A comedy troupe has to be funny on an island where even the accountants are wiseacres.

There's Dagwood's Diner and the Fritz Hug and Field Mouse Art Gallery and Belcher Bob's Bakery Eatery Scenery.

And then there's Blaster Dave.

Dave's Drilling and Blasting, actually. Dave's motto in the phone book: We Don't Stand Behind Our Work — We Stand Behind a Tree.

Dave doesn't sound like your average dynamite jockey. But then, nobody on the whole blinkin' island seems terribly average. Still, Blaster Dave — he's in a class by himself.

Blaster Dave has even got an auxiliary, back-up motto printed here in the phone book. It reads: People Swear by Us — They Call Up Dave and Say BLASPHEMY.

I think even the archbishop of Canterbury would get a chortle out of that one.

Taking It All Off

The nude thing. Let me try to tell you what it's like to sit bare-butted on a log on a beach talking to a woman you've just met who also just happens to be naked as a jay bird.

Easy. It felt easy.

There was Judy Williams, chairman of the Wreck Beach Preservation Society, and there was I . . . on Wreck Beach, a stretch of sand about twenty, twenty-five minutes from downtown Vancouver that just happens to be "clothing optional." Flesh to the left of us, flesh to the right of us. Acres and acres of burnished human flesh basting in the sun.

I don't come to such a situation easily, you know. Mine was a conventional, rural, southern Ontario, Louis St. Laurent-era upbringing, which is to say restrained . . . muffled . . . thwarted like a Japanese bonsai.

Were we taught that sex was dirty? No. We weren't taught that sex was anything. Sex was unimaginable. But bare flesh . . . *that* was pretty dirty.

I remember my Grade 8 teacher, Miss Sanford, wearing a slightly low-cut blouse one day. She leaned over to dump the shavings from the pencil sharpener in the wastebasket, betraying just a whisker of cleavage for no more than a millisecond.

Turned my knees to porridge.

I remember Mary Jane Chapman jogging doggedly around the high-school track one Thursday afternoon wearing those stupid baggy blue bloomers they made all the girls wear. Sad sacks that would make Sharon Stone look like a couch potato. My throat was so dry I couldn't swallow.

I lived through the age of the maxi, the midi, and the glory hallelu-jah mini skirt . . . watching that hem go up, up, way up . . . scarcely believing my luck at being alive and not blind.

No, I don't come lightly or nonchalantly to the sight of exposed female flesh. And yet . . . and yet. There I was, sitting naked on a log on Wreck Beach, talking to naked Judy Williams. And not blushing or giggling or ebbing or flowing. Feeling totally at ease.

As a matter of fact, it occurred to me that I felt even more at ease than if I'd been wearing a bathing suit. Because if I'd been wearing a bathing suit, I probably would have been conned into the old macho mug's game of trying to look fit. Sucking in my gut, puffing out my chest. When you're buck naked, surrounded by every conceivable variety of other naked people, there's no point in bluffing. People see what you are, so you might as well relax.

And I did. That was the greatest thing about being starkers on Wreck Beach. Aside from feeling the sun and the wind on parts of my body where I'd never felt the sun and wind before. I felt totally relaxed.

And yet . . . and yet . . .

Call me twisted. Call me an incorrigible old throwback to my uptight, priggish, and puritanical upbringing, but I have to confess that as Judy and I packed up after our talk and she turned to go up the path ahead of me, I couldn't stop my eyes from casting a furtive glance at her, couldn't stop my mind from muttering, "I wonder what she looks like with her clothes on?"

Walk, Don't Run

Great news, folks! It looks like the world of personal exercise is finally returning to the realm of sanity. If you'd care to jump on the sweat-stained bandwagon, here's what you do:

- Throw away your Spandex tights.
- Put your stationary exercise bike in a garage sale.
- Sell your chest expanders, your Pow-R-Grips, your ankle weights, and your Joe-Weider-How-to-Look-Like-Schwarznegger-in-Ninety-Days video.
- Let cobwebs grow on your Nautilus. Give your barbells to that lout of a nephew who's probably gobbling steroids anyway. Have your $180 cross-training shoes bronzed and plant geraniums in them.

You don't need that stuff any more, because Walking Is In.

Yep, just plain and simple walking. No special sunglasses, no Gortex jumpsuit, no ultra-lite fibreglass poles. All you need is a comfortable pair of shoes and a sense of curiosity.

You can burn as many calories walking for an hour as you can busting your lungs running laps around the track. The difference is that with walking, you don't end up feeling like you've been hit by a speeding laundry van.

Some folks are serious walkers. Take Jack Hitt. Jack's a guy who makes his living as a scribbler in darkest downtown New York. A couple of years ago he decided he needed to get away from it all, so he flew to France, bought a packsack, and started walking.

Eight hundred miles and two mountain ranges later, he pulled up in Santiago de Compostela, which is pretty much as far as you can go in northwestern Spain without tumbling into the Atlantic Ocean.

Jack had retraced the route taken by Christian pilgrims back in medieval times — and he'd done it step by gruelling step.

Lots of folks see Spain and France from an air-conditioned seat in a tour bus, or through the windshield of a rented car. Seeing it on foot is a whole different experience and a fascinating one. You can read about it in Hitt's book *Off the Road: A Modern-Day Walk Down the Pilgrims' Route into Spain*. It's published by Simon and Shuster.

Ffyona Campbell hasn't written a book yet, but I'll bet she's going to. She'll probably get down to it as soon as she finishes soaking her feet.

Ffyona ambled into John O'Groats late one afternoon recently. John O'Groats is as far north as you can go in Britain without tumbling into the North Sea.

Mind you, Ffyona had been there before. In 1983, as a matter of fact, when she walked *out* of John O'Groats.

In the eleven years in between her visits, Ffyona had walked. And walked and walked and walked. From the top of Britain to Land's End at the bottom. Then, just for good measure, she strolled across Europe. And Africa. And Asia. And Australia. And then she walked from New York to Los Angeles.

"I just wanted to see how far I could go," the twenty-seven-year-old woman explained. Adventures on the way? Belie**ve** it. It took her nearly two years to get across Africa, including a near-rape in Morocco and a political riot in Zaire.

Was it worth it? Well, it got her in *The Guinness Book of Records* as the first woman to walk around the world.

In terms of personal rewards, I've seen a photograph of Ffyona Campbell. She's as slim as an ultra-marathoner, looks very fit and ruddy. And appears to have great legs.

Ffyona's adventure will never win her any speed records. She took eleven years to make the trek, including several breaks to go back home and earn some more travelling money.

Guinness credits American William Kunst with the fastest walk around the world. Kunst left his home in Minnesota in 1970 and set a blistering pace, arriving back at his starting point in a mere four years. Ffyona took nearly three times that long.

But then, that's the whole pleasure of walking as an exercise — there's no big hurry.

Off Roading

Do you realize Jack Kerouac's been dead for more than thirty years? Man, that makes you feel old. Doesn't seem like three decades since our parents were poo-pooing and tut-tutting those "crazy beatnik bohemians" and a lot of us suburban angsters were secretly wondering if we could get our mitts on a beret and some bongos.

The Beat Generation had a special cachet for Canucks because, hey, the patron saint was one of us. Oh, sure, Kerouac was born in Lowell, Massachusetts, but that didn't make him American. Mais non. Canadien. Français. Kerouac himself once said, "All my knowledge rests in my French Canadianness and nowhere else."

No doubt about it, Kerouac was as Canadian as Mounties, maple syrup, and Mackenzie King.

And I'm not sure that King and Kerouac wouldn't have got along pretty well if they'd met. Politically they were both a couple of votes short of a quorum.

It's ironic that Kerouac was adopted as the philosophical darling of the American left, because politically he was about as left-wing as Ralph Kramden. His biographer, Ann Charters, writes, "Kerouac tried LSD once. With Timothy Leary at Harvard in 1961. After this experience with LSD, Kerouac was sure it had been introduced into America by the Russians as part of a plot to weaken the country. . . .

"Kerouac couldn't join forces with the Liberal Left," continues Charters, "and he couldn't attend the conservatives' fund-raising dinners . . . so he found himself caught in the middle. There was only one solution: to drop out in the great tradition of Thoreau, Mark Twain and Daniel Boone."

And so drop out he did. Kerouac went on the road and wrote

On the Road and compelled a goodly chunk of a generation to at least dream of following him down the gravel shoulder of that never-ending undulating highway.

In *On The Road,* Kerouac wrote this: "The only people for me are the mad ones, the ones who are mad to live, mad to talk, mad to be saved . . . the ones who never yawn and say a commonplace thing, but burn, burn, burn, like fabulous yellow roman candles exploding like spiders across the stars."

We kids ate that stuff up. Others didn't. The author Truman Capote sneered, "That's not writing, that's typing."

Maybe. But I have a hunch that Kerouac jolted — and continues to jolt — a lot more readers than Capote ever will.

They both ended badly. Capote lisping society gossip between commercials on late-night talk shows, Kerouac worse than that. Slumped on a day couch in a booze haze amid a welter of beer cans in a Florida trailer park. Watching daytime TV. With his mother.

A lot of larger-than-life types end badly. Joe Louis wound up as a coked-out celebrity greeter at the door of a Las Vegas gambling casino. The great Chairman Mao, it turns out, wasn't so great. He was an ageing lecher with green teeth, industrial strength BO, and a penchant for deflowering young party maidens from the hinterlands. Nixon was a crook and Brezhnev had the mental acuity of a fire hydrant and Mackenzie King, of course, chatted with his shaving mirror and consulted his dog before he talked to the Cabinet. There's a lesson for mere mortals in all this . . . a lesson we've already heard from a gypsy-troubadour type who, back in the sixties, hit the highway and hopped the freights and generally did a lot of the things that Jack Kerouac did in his prime. "Don't follow leaders," the gypsy troubadour advised.

Bob Dylan said that.

Who, come to think of it, has been looking more than a little shaky himself of late.

Elevator Elegy

Question time, sodbusters: what's the first word that springs to mind when somebody mentions the Canadian Prairies?

Lots of possibilities. If you've ever driven off a Prairie road and found your car up to its leaf springs in a dark brown goop with a constituency somewhere between molasses and Portland cement, the word "gumbo" might sum up the experience for you.

For others, the word "grasslands" might do it — although it's a pretty wussy word to describe the billowing, endless ocean of green and yellow that stretches from horizon to horizon and beyond.

Some folks think "gophers" when they think of our West. Or maybe "sunsets" (sub-section: spectacular).

For me, it's elevators. Those austere and elegant wooden high-rises that have dotted the Prairies for more than a century. Sometimes, when you're driving across the Prairies, a grain elevator is all you *can* see. And you see it for hours, rearing up out of the flatlands, just up the road apiece, tantalizing you. It's amazing how long you can see a Prairie elevator before you reach it.

The first ones went up in the 1880s. They were convenient places to store wheat crops along the railway lines. All the farmers in a district would haul their grain down to the elevator and "pool" it with their neighbours' crops. Pretty soon a general store would go up, then a livery and maybe a café. Before long, a little cluster of buildings had hunkered down around the elevator.

How many Prairie towns were seeded that way? Hundreds, perhaps thousands. They didn't all become big or even middling places, but they were there. People farmed and fought and prayed and played and loved and lived and died in those tiny settlements.

And none of that would have happened without the elevator.

I visited one such town last summer — Piapot, in Saskatchewan. Piapot is just off the Trans-Canada Highway, roughly halfway between Swift Current and Medicine Hat, Alberta.

It's a wonderful town, full of characters who look and act like they walked straight out of a W.O. Mitchell novel.

It's a fascinating town, but it's dying.

It thrived back in the middle years of the century. Now the population has shrivelled to forty-three — many of them old-timers planning to leave for a town with a doctor when their health starts to fail.

Trouble is, there's not much to do in Piapot now that the train doesn't stop there any more.

And now another nail in the coffin. The Piapot grain elevator is scheduled to close.

It's a depressingly familiar story on the Prairies these days. There's a contractor by the name of Don Wilcox who has spent the past fifteen years pulling down grain elevators all across Saskatchewan.

It wasn't Don's idea — the Saskatchewan Wheat Pool hired him to do it. Saskatchewan wheat farmers are consolidating — moving their crops into huge centralized concrete bunkers that can hold one hundred times the volume of those rickety old wooden elevators.

The new structures aren't called elevators. They're called marketing centres.

It's progress — but it's death for the old-style elevators, and death for the communities that flourished around them.

So far, Don Wilcox and his demolition crew have felled nearly a thousand wooden elevators across Saskatchewan. They expect to have the species fully exterminated in the next few years.

Some will survive, preserved as tourist attractions, souvenir shops, or funky little chamber of commerce offices.

Maybe some entrepreneur will tart them up and sell some of them off as weekend retreats for yuppie lawyers from Regina and Moose Jaw and Winnipeg.

The poet A.M. Klein wrote a poem about a grain elevator once:

Up . . .
it rises blind and Babylonian
like something out of legend.

That's what our Prairie elevators have become, all right — something out of legend.

I wonder if anybody will ever write a poem about the new Prairie marketing centres?

Black Like Yours Truly

In America, only the successful writer is important. In France, all writers are important. In England, no writer is important. In Australia, you have to explain what a writer is.

GEOFFREY COTTERELL

And in Canada? What of the Great White Frozen Attic? What's it like to be a professional writer in Canada?

Well, as a scribbler who's kept the bailiffs at bay for thirty-odd years by wielding nothing more lethal than a single-action Olivetti, I'd have to say Canadian writers fall somewhere between the American and Australian extremes. Which is to say that successful writers (Margaret Atwood, Robertson Davies, Alice Munro, Mordecai Richler) don't exactly have to take in laundry to make ends meet. On the other hand, they can still pilot their own grocery cart down at the local supermarket without worrying about being mobbed by groupies in the frozen-food section.

People have a lot of misconceptions about the writing business. The biggest delusion is that writing for a living will make you rich. Not likely. If you envision a life of wallowing in megabucks in the back seat of a chauffeur-driven stretch limo, best you try some other line of work — like mugging or high seas piracy or criminal law. Most writers in Canada are lucky to keep their noses above the poverty line.

Another major misconception about writing is that it is somehow easy, romantic, and fun. It is to whimper ruefully. There's nothing fun or romantic about sitting down in front of a blank piece of paper or a vacant computer screen day after day. And easy? It looks that way only when it's done well.

If you ever want to have your nose rearranged without benefit of plastic surgery, get yourself introduced to a writer and say, "Yeah, but what do you *really* do for a living?"

A brain surgeon once cornered Margaret Laurence at a literary cocktail party and trumpeted, "So you're an author! That's great! You know, when I retire from medicine, I'm going to be an author!"

Margaret Laurence looked at him through those hooded eyes, took a drag on her ever-present cigarette, and replied softly: "Fascinating. And when I retire, I plan to take up brain surgery."

Now, don't misunderstand me — I don't want to make writing sound like the root canal of career choices. It's not. The only real dangers in this line of work are nasty critics, unreasonable editors, and the odd paper cut.

Oh, yes . . . and there is the ego problem.

It doesn't happen often, but once in a while your typical Canadian author will become somewhat . . . full of himself. Put on airs. Act like he or she is actually important.

Happened to me not long ago. I'd just published my fifth book and decided that, dammit, real writers don't go around in T-shirts, jeans, and baseball caps. Chap in my position ought to look more . . . well, *authorly*. So I went out and bought a tweed jacket, complete with side vents and suede elbow patches.

I felt like Pierre Berton by way of Robertson Davies with a touch of Farley Mowat in my new threads. On an impulse, I sashayed into a bookstore, briskly rapped the bell, and asked the startled clerk if they carried "that new book by Black."

"Who?" the clerk asked blankly.

"Black. Arthur Black. Clever fellow. Probably in your Canadiana section. Or perhaps under World Humour . . ."

The clerk had never heard of him (me). And neither had his computer.

"This is intolerable!" I blustered. "The man has written five books. Surely a bookstore this large would have at least one of them!"

The clerk searched and searched. And finally, deep in the second-hand racks, just beside the remainders bin, he came up with one dog-eared, bookworm-riddled copy of my first book, *Basic Black*.

My book had been filed, along with books by Dick Gregory, H. Rap Brown, a biography of Mohammed Ali, and the collected speeches of Martin Luther King, under Black Revolutionary Studies.

Sniping: A Canadian Specialty

I think I've finally identified the crazy glue that keeps this lanky, loose-jointed lug of a country of ours together.

It's our hatred for each other.

Well, not "hatred" exactly. Disaffection maybe. Or even antipathy. Snootiness. Whatever it is that makes Canucks so enthusiastic about tearing strips off one another.

We do it all the time. And no corner of the country goes unscathed. Leave aside the eternal cat fight between Quebec and the rest of us. Never mind the Western exasperation with the East, or the Northern resentment of the South — let's get specific.

Montreal on Toronto: "Congratulations! You have won first prize: a week in Toronto. Second prize: two weeks in Toronto."

And Toronto? Toronto hates Edmonton. Well, Mel Lastman does. A while back, the dubiously coiffed mayor called Edmonton "a clapboard outhouse." Did Edmontonians notice? Not hardly. They were too busy cracking wise about *their* urban peeve, Calgary. "What's the difference between a pigeon and a Calgarian? A pigeon can still make deposits on a Buick."

Westerners have a knack for this blood sport. Here's a Saskatonian taking aim at Regina: "The best way to see Regina . . . is through a double martini at 35,000 feet."

And then there's Winnipeg. Poor Winnipeg. One of my favourite, largely unsung, Canadian cities — but you'd never be able to explain it from the press it gets. A hundred years ago Bob Edwards, acerbic editor of the *Calgary EyeOpener,* got off the train in Winnipeg and wrote, "So this is Winnipeg — I can tell it ain't Paris."

A century later, Winnipeg fares no better in the Canadian cosmopolitan consciousness. Recently, the *Montreal Gazette,* in a fit of civic boosterism, ran a series of articles plumping life in Montreal. Part of the self-promotion included this typically hipper-than-thou Canadian qualifier: "If after reading this in-depth series on Montreal, you're still undecided — perhaps you need a week in Winnipeg."

It goes on everywhere. The *Globe and Mail* looks at Vancouver and sniffs: "Lovely and lazy and famous and marginal." Vancouver slags Victoria: "God's waiting room," they call it. Nova Scotia slags Newfoundland: "A piece of rock entirely surrounded by fog." The Newfies volley back with "Nova Scotia: A peninsula entirely surrounded by fish." (Well, it's an old joke.)

A few weeks ago, I was in Nelson, B.C., a beautiful town in the towering Kootenays. A place with no need to strut its stuff because its stuff is so eminently, obviously heavenly.

So what's the first thing I hear in Nelson? A joke about Castlegar, eighteen miles down the road. "What's the difference between Castlegar and a cup of yogurt? A cup of yogurt has a live culture."

Regional backbiting — Canada's Olympic sport. When I lived in Fergus, Ontario, I was a southerner. Except to folks in London and Windsor, who considered me a northerner. When I moved to Thunder Bay, I *became* a northerner. Well, to everybody in Toronto. To Yellowknifers and Whitehorsians, I was still a limp-wristed, Tilley-jacketed, southern gawkhammer. And everybody west of Kenora dismissed me as a carpet-bagging, money-grubbing Easterner fresh from the flesh pots of Bay Street.

What *is* it about us? We come from all over the globe to settle in this last best piece of real estate on the planet . . . and then we turn into snipers. "You settled *there?* Oh, no . . . I settled *here.* Much nicer . . . and here's a one-liner to prove it."

What we really need is a generic, all-inclusive wisecrack, a catchphrase that captures the essence of all of us who wound up in this permafrosted corral north of the forty-ninth. The raggedy-assed Scots and the potato-blighted Irish; the indentured French, disgruntled Germans and Finns and Basques and Serbs; the war-weary Asians, expat Yankees, disaffected Aussies and Austrians and Argentinans; and of course the first people, the Innu, the Inuit, the Inishinabe, who watched us Johnny-, Jacques-, and Juan-come-latelies with a stoic glint in their landlord eye. How about a catch-phrase? A one-liner. Hell, even a one-*worder* that encompasses the essence of all those some-times crazy, frequently desperate dreamers who decided, for a thousand different reasons, to call this place home.

How be we call them . . . Canadians?

"Yanking" Our Chain

So how does it feel to be an American?

Don't go all huffy on me. You're an American. So am I. We all are. Geographically speaking, anyway. And if you don't like it, don't blame me. Blame Martin Waldseemuller. The German cartographer gave us the term nearly 500 years ago. And when he said "America," he wasn't talking about Dubuque or Okefenokee or the Upper West Side. He meant the whole danged New World, from Tierra del Fuego to the North Pole.

Five centuries can change things a lot. And they have. If Martin Waldseemuller had had his way, Chileans, Brazilians, Panamanians, Saskatonians, and Georgia Crackers would all be known collectively as Americans today . . . but it hasn't worked out that way. Nope. We are North Americans, South Americans, Central Americans — or, for those who happened to be born in the upper middle layer of the sandwich — Americans.

It gets worse, as any Canuck who's travelled in Europe can tell you. Open your mouth to ask for a pint of Watney's Red Barrel in Britain and the barman is likely to counter with "Wot part of the States are you from, mate?"

Ride the métro in Paris with a Nikon slung around your neck and you're almost certain to hear mutters of "*maudit Americain!*"

I remember a stilted tiff I had years ago with a Spanish guide who insisted I was Americano. I told him no, I was Canadian. He smirked back, "But you live in Nort' America, no? *Pues, Americano.*"

I asked him if that meant it was okay for me to refer to him as *Portugueso*.

I think that's the only argument I ever won in Spain.

Maybe it's a lesson in humility for Canadians. It gives us an idea how the Scots, the Irish, and the Welsh must feel when we blithely refer to Britain when we mean England; how miffed the Dutch must be when we talk about their country as Holland. (Holland is no more a country than the Okanagan Valley is a province.)

Still, nobody passed a law giving the Yanks exclusive world rights to the term "American" — and I'd like to have it back, at least as an option.

And I think we can make a case of historical precedent. Consider the British (sorry, English) poet John Donne. Mr. Donne was thinking expansively when he wrote a poem to his mistress, calling her "O my America! my new-found-land."

I like to believe he was thinking of Come by Chance at the time.